PYTHON
CRASH COURSE FOR
DATA ANALYSIS

A Complete Beginner's Guide
for Python Coding, NumPy, Pandas
and Data Visualization

AI PUBLISHING

How to Contact Us

If you have any feedback, please let us know by sending an email to contact@aispublishing.net.

Your feedback is immensely valued, and we look forward to hearing from you. It will be beneficial for us to improve the quality of our books.

To get the Python codes and materials provided with this book, please click to the link below:

https://www.aispublishing.net/python-crash-course-da

About the Publisher

At AI Publishing Company, we have established an international learning platform specifically for young students, beginners, small enterprises, startups, and managers who are new to data sciences and artificial intelligence.

Through our interactive, coherent, and practical books and courses, we help beginners learn skills that are crucial to developing AI and data science projects.

Our courses and books range from basic introduction courses to language programming and data sciences to advanced courses for machine learning, deep learning, computer vision, big data, and much more, using programming languages like Python, R, and some data science and AI software.

AI Publishing's core focus is to enable our learners to create and try proactive solutions for digital problems by leveraging the power of AI and data sciences to the maximum extent.

Moreover, we offer specialized assistance in the form of our free online content and eBooks, providing up-to-date and useful insight into AI practices and data science subjects, along with eliminating the doubts and misconceptions about AI and programming.

Our experts have cautiously developed our online courses and kept them concise, short, and comprehensive so that you can understand everything clearly and effectively and start practicing the applications right away.

We also offer consultancy and corporate training in AI and data sciences for enterprises so that their staff can navigate through the workflow efficiently.

With AI Publishing, you can always stay closer to the innovative world of AI and data sciences.

If you are eager to learn the A to Z of AI and data sciences but have no clue where to start, AI Publishing is the finest place to go.

Please contact us by email at: contact@aispublishing.net.

AI Publishing Is Looking for Authors Like You

Interested in becoming an author for AI Publishing? Please contact us at author@aispublishing.net.

We are working with developers and AI tech professionals just like you, to help them share their insights with the global AI and Data Science lovers. You can share all your knowledge about hot topics in AI and Data Science.

Download the Color Images

We request you to download the PDF file containing the color images of the screenshots/diagrams used in this book here:

https://www.aispublishing.net/python-crash-course-da

Get in Touch with Us

Feedback from our readers is always welcome.

For general feedback, please send us an email at contact@aipublishing.net and mention the book title in the subject line.

Although we have taken extraordinary care to ensure the accuracy of our content, errors do occur. If you have found an error in this book, we would be grateful if you could report this to us as soon as you can.

If you are interested in becoming an AI Publishing author and if you have expertise in a topic and you are interested in either writing or contributing to a book, please send us an email at author@aipublishing.net.

Book Approach

This book presumes that you know nothing about Python coding. Its primary goal is to present you with the concepts, the ideas, the intuitions, and the elementary tools you need to actually start coding and analyzing data in Python.

While you can read this book without switching on your laptop, we highly recommend you experiment with the practical aspects.

You will find all the materials provided with this book: Python codes, references, exercises, and extra PDF contents at:

https://www.aispublishing.net/python-crash-course-da

About the Author

I like to identify myself as a lover of all the incredible ways science can change the world. My name is Fernando Henrique Fernandes. I am a Data Scientist and I apply Machine Learning techniques in my researches. I am experienced in EDA, the creation of ML/DL models, and Data acquisition. Additionally, I have the certification as a Data Scientist and Analyst, completed the Deep Learning Specialization on Deep Learning, AI and Deep Learning.

Feel free to contact me. Here is my Github and my LinkedIn.

Table of Contents

1

Introduction to Python and Data Analysis

This book works as a guide to present fundamental concepts, theory, examples, and hands-on projects related to Data Analysis using Python. In this first chapter, an overall look of the book objectives and its format will be presented.

1.1. Who Is This Book for?

This book is for anyone genuinely interested in Data Analysis. It contains crucial definitions, theoretical explanations, presentation of tools, as well as direct examples and tutorials. The requirements of this book are a basic understanding of the following Subjects:

- Mathematics
- Programming
- Statistics

If you don't feel at ease with any of these subjects, do not worry. An explanation for beginners will always be provided along this book, as well as further sources. The language utilized in this book is Python, and there are some chapters dedicated to the language applied.

1.2. Why Python?

First, Python is a high-level multi-purpose interpreted language. It is well established and focuses on code readability and ease of use. Furthermore, there are innumerable packages and libraries available for Python, from scientific ones to big data specific. All these libraries, combined with Python's easy learning curve, make this language an incredible tool with great versatility.

Some examples of packages related to Data Analysis and Machine Learning presented in Python include:

- Numpy
- Pandas
- Scipy
- Matplotlib
- Seaborn
- Bokeh
- Scikit-Learn
- TensorFlow
- Pytorch

These are some of the packages, but many others could be listed.

Additionally, according to Stack Overflow, Python has the largest number of questions when compared to the other major programming languages. This can be shown in the graph below.

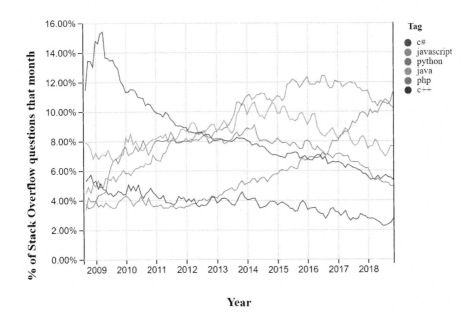

Year

The graph also shows how rapidly this growth happened throughout the years, and that this trend is not slowing down. Therefore, Python is the appropriate language for this book. The version of Python used and referred to in this book is Python 3 because Python 2 is deprecated and soon will not be supported.

1.3. How to Use This Book?

This book is filled with definitions of methods, tools, and algorithms. The book is clearly organized into chapters that cover all the basic concepts and packages used by a Data Analyst using Python. Each chapter will cover a topic in detail and possibly present exercises and applied projects when applicable.

Frequently, you will encounter three types of box-tags in this book: Requirements, **Further Readings,** and **Hands-on Time.** Examples of these boxes are shown below.

Requirements

This box lists all requirements needed to be done before proceeding to the next topic. Generally, it works as a checklist to see if everything is ready before a tutorial.

Further Readings

Here, you will be pointed to some external reference or source that will serve as additional content about the specific Topic being studied. In general, it consists of packages, documentations, and cheat sheets.

Hands-on Time

Here, you will be pointed to an external file to train and test all the knowledge acquired about a Tool that has been studied. Generally, these files are Jupyter notebooks (.ipynb), Python (.py) files or documents (.pdf).

The Requirements tag is there to remind you of the steps needed to be performed after a specific tutorial or topic. **Further Readings** works as a great form of a more detailed and in-depth reference for specific topics. While **Hands-on Time** should work as a break from the flow of the book and prepare you to start working directly using the presented tool. All box tags are important, and it is highly recommended that you follow their instructions.

1.4. What is Data Analysis?

In short, Data Analysis is the process of making sense of data. Generally, to achieve this goal, multiple steps are required, such as data inspection, cleaning, transforming, combining, and modeling. In today's business, it has a crucial role in the decision-making process.

According to the statistician, John Tukey, Data Analysis is defined as: "Procedures for analyzing data, techniques for interpreting the results of such procedures, ways of planning the gathering of data to make its analysis easier, more precise or more accurate, and all the machinery and results of (mathematical) statistics which apply to analyzing data."

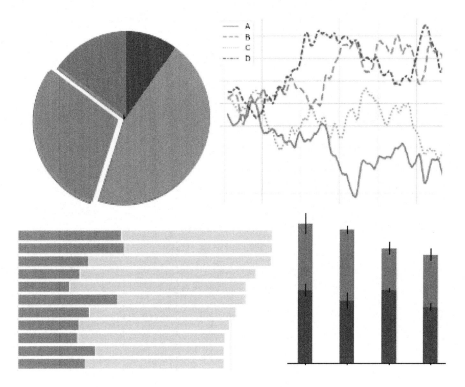

Therefore, the main objective of a Data Analyst is to make an optimal decision based on existing data that supports it. A Data Analysis should be capable of manipulating and preparing the data, so it can produce the desired insight. This insight can be communicated or reported using graphs, reports, and visualizations that will facilitate the decision-making process.

2

Getting Started

This chapter will discuss all the needed steps to have an environment up and running. Therefore, we will go into the details about the most common installation processes for all the technologies utilized right through the book. Additionally, we will describe the basic concepts of Anaconda Distribution and package managers. All these topics should cover the steps needed for the initial set-up and packages installation.

2.1. Installing Python

There are three main ways to download and install Python 3.

1. Official Python Website: This installation method is the most common and fastest. However, if you install Python this way, each external library and packages will have to be installed separately. **Therefore, this method is not recommended**.

2. Miniconda: This installer contains the **conda** package manager and Python. Once installed, you can use the *Anaconda Prompt* to install other packages and create environments. Like the previous method, each package installation will have to be done manually.

3. Anaconda Distribution: This method includes all the packages used in this book and many others. Therefore, this is the **recommended installation process**. The downside of this installation is that it requires a large file to be downloaded that may not be ideal, depending on your internet speed and bandwidth restrictions.

In all cases, you should download **version 3** of Python, which the most current version and is already widely used and supported by third-party libraries.

Please keep in mind that only one installation process is necessary. You should choose the one that is most adequate for you based on their description above. In general, options 1 and 2 are more appropriate for slow/limited internet connections or low disk space, and option 3 is ideal if there are no internet/ storage restrictions.

Below, there is a small step-by-step installation guide for all the options cited previously.

§ Download Python from the Official Website

1. On the *downloads* page of the official Python website https://www.python.org/downloads/, your operating

system should be automatically detected and the download option available.

2. If your Operational System is correct, just click on the **Download Python** Button. Otherwise, select one OS in the options below.

3. After clicking, your download should start right away. Just run the installer and follow the installation process as any other program.

§ Miniconda

Miniconda

	Windows	Mac OS X	Linux
Python 3.7	64-bit (exe installer)	64-bit (bash installer)	64-bit (bash installer)
	32-bit (exe installer)	64-bit (.pkg installer)	32-bit (bash installer)
Python 2.7	64-bit (exe installer)	64-bit (bash installer)	64-bit (bash installer)
	32-bit (exe installer)	64-bit (.pkg installer)	32-bit (bash installer)

1. Choose the appropriate OS on the following URL https:// docs.conda.io/en/latest/miniconda.html and click on the download button. As always, the download should start, and you can proceed to follow the installation process.

§ Anaconda Distribution

Anaconda 2018.12 for Windows Installer

1. The download section of the Anaconda Distribution for all operating systems is available at https://www.anaconda. com/distribution/#download-section, select your OS.

2. Click **Download** for the version 3, and the download should start right away. Run the installer after the download is completed, and follow the instructions.

2.2. Packages, Managers, and Repositories

Once more, there two main sources of Python packages: **PyPI** and **Anaconda Repo**. Both can be used to install packages and are very popular for doing it. Now, let's look at each one of these package sources and how to install software using them.

> ### Hands-on Time – Running Commands in Your OS
> To run any command of the package managers, you need to know how to run command line commands. There is a small tutorial to check if you can run commands in the terminal of different OS. The instructions are in the file **system_commands.pdf**.

2.2.1. PyPI and PIP

According to their <u>website</u>, "The Python Package Index (PyPI) is a repository of software for the Python programming language." In other words, it contains a collection of software developed and distributed by the community. Additionally, it provides a convenient and easy way to install these packages and their dependencies, **pip**.

- **PIP: pip is the Python package installer that can be used to install packages in PyPI.**

You may be asking yourself, "Ok, so I need this pip to install packages from this index. But how do I install pip?" Do not worry, since Python 3.4 pip comes with Python. Therefore, if you have Python installed, you should be able to use it.

Now, let's check some commands of the **pip**.

§ PIP Commands

The most common commands used to manage packages using **pip** is listed below.

o Install Packages

To install any package from the PyPI, you just need to type the command below:

```
pip install package_name
```

If you want a particular version of the package:

```
pip install package_name==version_number
```

Install packages listed in a requirements file:

```
pip install -r requirements.txt
```

o Search Packages

Search packages available at **PyPI**:

```
pip search search_query
```

o List Installed Packages

List all the locally available packages and their versions:

```
pip list
```

o Update Installed Packages

If you want to update an installed package:

```
pip install package_name --upgrade
```

o Uninstall Packages

If you want to remove a package:

```
pip uninstall package_name
```

o Save Installed Packages in Requirements File

If you want to create the requirements file with all the current packages installed:

```
pip freeze > requirements.txt
```

OBS: The file created by this command can only be used by pip, not conda.

2.2.2. Anaconda Repo and Conda

Anaconda Repo is a package repository like **PyPI**. It lists all the packages available in the Anaconda Distribution. In order to install the packages available in this repository, there is the **conda:** a package and environment manager. Although there is some overlap between the functionality of **pip** and **conda**, the latter has more functionalities, such as the management of environments, no need for compilers during installation, and not being limited to Python software.

- **Conda: conda is an environment and package manager that can be used to install packages from Anaconda Repo.**

As said previously, **conda** is more than a package manager. It is also an environment manager. Sometimes, you want to create an isolated environment for your project. This is the purpose of the environment capabilities of **conda**. Each environment works as a new isolated installation of Python that can have its own dependencies. This way, you can have multiple environments, each with certain packages installed.

Further Readings – Conda

If you want to know more details on how to use **conda**, check its documentation. Additionally, for quick reference, you could check this cheat sheet available on their site.

Now, let's check some of **conda**'s commands.

Requirements – Conda Commands

- Conda is only available if you used the options **2-Miniconda** or **3-Anaconda Distribution** during installation.

- The commands below should be executed in the **Anaconda Prompt**, which will be available after installation.

- **Package Manager Commands** will affect only the currently **active environment**.

§ Conda Package Managing Commands

Below, there is a list of the most common commands used to manage packages in the current active conda environment.

o Install Packages

To install packages from Anaconda Repo:

```
conda install package_name
```

If you want a particular version of the package:

```
conda install package_name=version_number
```

Install packages listed in a requirements file:

```
conda install --file requirements.txt
```

o Search Packages

Search packages available at **PyPI**:

```
conda search search_query
```

o List Installed Packages

List all the locally available packages and their versions:

```
conda list
```

o **Update Installed Packages**

If you want to update an installed package:

```
conda update package_name
```

o **Uninstall Packages**

If you want to remove installed package:

```
conda remove package_name
```

o **Save Installed Packages in Requirements file**

If you want to create the requirements file with all the current packages installed:

```
conda list -e > requirements.txt
```

OBS: The file created by this command can only be used by conda, not pip.

§ Conda Environment Managing Commands

As said previously, conda has the capability to handle different environments. Below, there is a list of the most common commands used to manage environments.

o **Create an Environment**

Create a new environment:

```
conda create --name environment_name
```

Create an environment from file:

```
conda env create --file file_name
```

o **Activate Environment**

Active a specific environment, on **OS X/Ubuntu**:

```
source activate environment_name
```

On **Windows**:

```
activate environment_name
```

o **List Environments**

List all environments:

```
conda env list
```

o **Remove an Environment**

If you want to remove an environment:

```
conda env remove --name environment_name
```

o **Save Environments in File**

Saves the current active environment as a YML file:

```
conda env export > file_name
```

Hands-on Time – Using pip/conda

Now, it is your turn. Follow the instructions in the **managing_ packages.pdf** to use pip/conda and exercise all the commands presented.

Python for
Data Analysis – Basics

Now that the software is ready, we can start to get used to the programming language. This chapter presents the basic concepts of Python, from variable declaration to the principles of the language. Therefore, we will go into the details of the basic syntax, flow control blocks, and intrinsic peculiarities. All these topics work as a presentation to the language for new users, or as a reminder for readers with good knowledge.

3.1. Python REPL

As soon as the Python installation is completed, you can immediately start to use it interactively using its Read Eval Print Loop (REPL). It works as a dynamics script in which you can create and modify variables and see instant results.

The main advantage of the REPL is that you can start experimenting right away. Therefore, it works as a great tool to test the basic syntax of the language. If any code is taking too long to run in the REPL, you may interrupt it with a ^C. This is considered a *runtime abort*.

§ Starting the REPL

To run it, you just need to or search for **Python** or type *python* in the command line:

```
Python
```

§ Interface

At first glance, it seems like just another CLI. Initially, it shows the basic information of the installed Python version.

```
Python 3.6.5 (v3.6.5:f59c0932b4, Mar 28 2018, 17:00:18) [MSC v.1900 64 bit (
AMD64)] on win32
Type "help", "copyright", "credits" or "license" for more information.
>>> ▂
```

§ Input Field

The input field is represented by the triple '>' symbol. This is where the commands/script should be typed.

```
>>>
```

Hands-on Time – Using Python REPL

Through the reading of the next topics, keep the **Python REPL** opened. Execute all the operators/commands presented to confirm its functionality yourself. Feel free to experiment other commands or combinations.

3.2. Python Basic - Data Types and Operators

Now, let's be familiar with all the basic types and operations of the language.

3.2.1. Comments

Any command starting with "#" is completely ignored.

```
>>> # This is just a comment
```

3.2.2. Basic Data Types

Like many programming languages, Python has all the standard data types implemented.

If you want to know the type of any object in Python, just use **type(object),** and the resulting type will be shown (which is a class in Python).

§ Numeric and Boolean Data Types

Type	Description	Examples
int	Integer type	354, 56, −42
float	Floating point type can be represented in scientific notation. 1e3 = 1x10^3=1000.	8.5, 0.0, −1.7e-5
bool	Boolean value	True, False

§ Strings

In Python, Strings are expressed in double ("...") or singles ('...') quotes. If you want to quote in your string, you can scape them using \, or use a different quote in its definition.

```
>>>»String»
'String'
```

```
>>>'»Hello»'
'»Hello»'
```

```
>>>»42»
'42'
```

```
>>>»can't»
«can't»
```

```
>>>'I\'m'
«I'm»
```

```
>>>'ABC123'
'ABC123'
```

Strings in python are represented by the class str. Python is different from some programming languages, and it doesn't have a character type. Therefore, a single character is also a string. Additionally, strings have many built-in methods that facilitate its manipulation and transformation. Most of these methods will be presented later in the book. Also, it should be noted that strings are immutable objects. Therefore, their values cannot be altered. If you want a different string, a new one should be created. You can cast different types of strings using the **str()** function.

```
PYTHON REPL:
>>> str(42)        # the string representation of integer 42
'42'
>>> str(.5)        # the string representation of float 0.5
'0.5'
```

§ None Type

The **None** keyword represents the **NoneType** in Python. It is a type that represents no values. In general, it is used to show that a function did not result in any values.

3.2.3. Variable Assignment

Assignment represents the binding of a name to a value or expression. As in multiple programming languages, variable assignment is done using the (=) operator. Variable names are case sensitive, and the keyword of the language cannot be used to represent variables names. You can have simple, multiple, and same values assignments.

```
PYTHON REPL:
>>> h = 'Hello'          # the string value "Hello"
                         is bind to name h
>>> H = 'Hi'             # the string value "Hi"
                         is bind to name H
>>> a = b = 2            # a and b are equal to 2
>>> c, d = 3, 4          # c and d are equal to 3 and 4,
                         respectively
```

3.2.4. Arithmetic Operators

Most arithmetic operators work just as expected between numeric values.

Operator	Description	Examples
+	Adds the 2 values	>>> 3 + 5 8
–	Subtracts the values	>>> 8 – 4 4
*	Multiply values	>>> 21 * 2 42
/	Divide the values, the returned values are always a float.	>>> 15 / 2 7.5
//	Floor division, it ignores any fractional values from results	>>> 15 / 2 7
%	Modulus, returns the remainder of the division	>>> 6 % 4 2
**	Raises to power	>>> 2**8 256
()	Ranks the order of operations	>>> (1 + 3) / 2 2.0

OBS$_1$.: Operations between bool and int/float are automatically converted to the numeric type (int/float) in which True is 1 and False is 0.

OBS$_2$.: Operations between float and int are automatically converted to float type.

OBS$_3$.: The operators + and * have a special effect on str type. For example:

```
PYTHON REPL:
>>>»hello» * 3
'hellohellohello'
>>>»ABC» + «DEF»
'ABCDEF'
```

As can be seen from the examples above, the str*int operation repeats the string values multiple times, and the str+str concatenates the strings.

§ Precedence and Associativity

Each operator has precedence in that expression. In other words, some operations are solved before the other. The order is shown in the table below:

Order	Operators	Description
1	()	Parentheses
2	**	Exponent
3	–x, +x	Unary minus or plus
4	*, /, //, %	Multiplication, division, floor division, modulus
5	+, –	Addition, subtraction

Operators with same precedence are solved by their associativity order.

Associativity	Operators	Example
Left-to-right	(), **, *, /, //, %, +, −	>>> 5/2%2 0.5
Right-to-left	**	>>> 2**2**3 256

This means that any expression will follow this order for resolution. First, the order in **Precedence Table**, then the order in **Associativity Table**.

§ Self-Increment

Multiple times, it is necessary to increment a variable. There is a small shortcut to perform this using the operators seen before. The shortcut operations and their representation are shown below.

Operator	Example	Equivalent Representation
+=	x += 2	x = x + 2
−=	x −= 3	x = x − 3
*=	x *= 4	x = x * 4
/=	x /= 5	x = x / 5
%/	x %= 6	x = x % 6

3.2.5. Comparison Operators

Values or expressions can be compared in Python using the comparison operators. The result of this assessment is a bool type.

Operators	Meaning	Example
>, <	Greater/lesser than	>>> 3 > 2 True
>=, <=	Greater/less than or equal	>>> 4 <= 2 + 2 True
==	Equal to	>>> 6 == 2 * 3 True
!=	Different of	>>> 3 != 3 False

OBS.: You can compare multiple things in Python, but be careful with the result of the comparison. For example, strings can be compared, but it results in the comparison between the ASCII values of their characters. Therefore, you need to be cautious when using these operators with non-numeric types.

§ Boolean Logic

When you want to combine multiple Boolean logic operations, you can use *and*, *or*, and *not* keywords. When used with Boolean values, operator *and* returns true only when both are true, operator *or* returns true when at least one is true, and the operator *not* inverts the Boolean value.

```
PYTHON REPL:
>>> 1 > 0 and 2 <= 4        # True and True is True
True
>>> 0 == 1 or 5 < 3         # False or False is False
'ABCDEF'
>>> not True                # Inverts bool value
False
```

3.3. Basic Containers – Lists and Tuples

There are two basic types of ordered sequences in Python: *list* and *tuple*. Both stores ordered values but have a crucial difference: mutability. While lists can be easily modified, tuples (just like strings) are immutable. Due to this difference, they are used in different cases. In general, `lists` are used when you need to modify, remove, or append values, while `tuples` are used when you only need to read the values. Thanks to the immutable restriction, iterations on `tuples` are faster than on `lists`.

3.3.1. Lists

As defined previously, lists are an ordered sequence of mutable values. They can contain multiple types of data. To define a `list`, you just need to write a sequence of comma-separated values between square brackets.

§ Defining Lists

Square brackets are used in list definitions.

```
PYTHON REPL:
>>> a = []                  # Empty list
>>> a = list()              # Empty list
>>> b = [1, 2, 3, 4, 5, 6]  # List with numeric values
>>> c = [42, 'hi', True]    # List with compound types
```

§ Function `list()`

Beyond creating an empty list, you can also create a list from previous objects such as strings.

```
PYTHON REPL:
>>> d = 'ABCDEF'                          # String
>>> list(d)                               # Converted to list
['A', 'B', 'C', 'D', 'E', 'F']
```

§ Indexing

Each value of the list is accessible by an index. The index represents the position of the value in the list, starting by position 0. Additionally, the negative index can be used counting from the end of the list. As lists are mutable, the index can also be used to change the values.

```
PYTHON REPL:
>>> b[0]                    # Accessing first value of b
1
>>> b[-1]                   # Accessing last value of b
6
>>> b[-3]                   # Accessing 3rd values
                              from the right of b
4
>>> c[2] = False            # Modifying the 3rd value of c
>>> c
[42, 'hi', False]
```

§ Slicing

Sometimes, instead of accessing a single value from a list, you may want to select a sub-list. For this, there is the slicing operation. Generally, slicing is used with [start:end] resulting in values from the start position until the end, the end position is excluded from the resulting substring. If omitted, the start defaults to 0 and the end to the length of the list. Furthermore, slicing can be used to change multiple values at once. The examples below show how slicing works.

```
PYTHON REPL:
>>> b[0:2]         # Values from position 0 to 2(excluded).
[1, 2]
>>> b[-3:-1]       # Values from -3 to -1(excluded)
[4, 5]
>>> b[:-2]         # Values from start to -2(excluded)
[1, 2, 3, 4]
>>> c[1:]          # All values from index 1 until the end
['hi', False]
>>> c[:]           # All values
[42, 'hi', False]
>>> c[0:2] = ['a', 'b'] # Change multiple values with
indexing
>>> c
['a', 'b', False]
```

A good way to create intuition about how slicing works is to think of the indexes as points between the values.

In the image above, slicing [−4:−1] returns [12, 13, 14] and [0:2] return [11, 12].

§ Concatenating and Repeating

Like strings, the operators + and * can be used to concatenate and repeat lists, respectively. The result is a new list. Additionally, **lists** have the method **append** that attaches a value to its end.

```
PYTHON REPL:
>>> [1, 2, 3] + [4, 5, 6]    # Concatenate lists together
[1, 2, 3, 4 ,5 ,6]
>>> [1, 2, 1] * 2            # Repeat List values
[1, 2, 1, 1, 2, 1]
>>> li = [1, 2, 3]
```

```
PYTHON REPL:
>>> li = [1, 2, 3]
>>> li.append(4)            # Append a value to the list end
>>> li
[1, 2, 3, 4]
```

3.3.2. Tuples

Tuples are immutable and can contain multiple types of data. Therefore, they are generally used to read static data.

§ Defining Tuples

Parenthesis are used to define tuples. To differentiate a tuple with a single value to a simple parenthesis expression, it must contain a comma. Examples:

```
PYTHON REPL:
>>> a = (,)                 # Empty Tuple
>>> t = (1,)                # Tuple with one value
>>> b = (1, 2, 3, 4, 5, 6)  # Tuple with numeric values
>>> c = (42, 'hi', True)    # Tuple with compound types
```

§ Function tuple()

Like lists, you can also create tuples from previous objects such as strings or lists.

```
PYTHON REPL:
>>> d = 'ABC'            # String
>>> e = [1, 2, 3]
>>> tuple(d)             # Converted to tuple
('A', 'B', 'C')
>>> tuple(e)             # Converted to tuple
(1, 2, 3)
```

§ Indexing

Just like lists, tuples can be indexed, and the same indexing rules are applied except for modifying its values. Examples:

```
PYTHON REPL:
>>> b[0]        # Accessing first value of b
1
>>> b[-1]       # Accessing last value of b
6
>>> b[-3]       # Accessing 3rd values from the right of b
4
>>> b[2] = 0    # Error tuples are immutable
TypeError: 'tuple' object does not support item assignment
```

§ Slicing

Tuples support slicing too; of course, not allowing change of the values.

```
PYTHON REPL:
>>> b[0:2]           # Values from position 0 to 2(excluded).
(1, 2)
>>> b[-3:- 1]        # Values from -3 to -1(excluded)
(4, 5)
>>> b[:-2]           # Values from start to -2(excluded)
(1, 2, 3, 4)
>>> c[1:]            # All values from index 1 until the end
(«hi», True)
>>> c[:]             # All values
(42, «hi», True)
```

§ Concatenating and Repeating

The operators + and * work as in lists. As tuples are not mutable, the result is a new tuple created from the concatenation or repetition. Examples:

```
PYTHON REPL:
>>> (1, 2, 3) + (4, 5, 6)     # New concatenated tuple
(1, 2, 3, 4 ,5 ,6)
>>> (1,2) * 2                 # New repeated tuple
(1, 2, 1, 2)
```

3.3.3. Function `len`

The **len** function can be used in most container types. It shows the number of elements in this container, whether a **list**, **tuple** or **string**. Some examples that show its usage:

PYTHON REPL:

```
>>> a, b, c = (42,), [1, 1], «abc»
>>>len(a)
1
>>>len(b)
2
>>>len(c)
3
```

3.4. Modules

The **Python REPL** is great for testing small code snippets and language syntax. However, after closed, all the variables and operations defined are lost. Therefore, to write longer programs and save the results, a text editor is necessary. In the editor, you can create a new file that contains the instructions and variable definitions. This file is called a script. Python scripts are saved with the **.py** extension.

Requirements - Text Editor

· One of the text editors presented in the Getting Started Chapter should be installed.

§ Running Scripts

Consider a script called **myscript.py**. In order to run this script, follow these instructions:

1. Open your system terminal.

2. Navigate to the script folder (where the **myscript.py** file is located).

3. Run the command:

```
python myscript.py
```

After all code in the script will be executed in the current terminal window, try to run the examples below. Paste their code in the text editor and save as example1.py and example2. py files. Then follow the instructions above to see the code outputs.

Example 1 - example1.py
# This is a comment
a = 5
print(a)
OUTPUT
5

Example 2 - example2.py
# This is a comment
b = 21 * 2
print(b)
OUTPUT
42

After invoking the modules, their instructions will be executed.

OBS.: In Visual Studio Code, the script could be executed directly in the IDE using the run button.

3.5. Conditional Statements

Like other languages, the code under the **if** statement is only executed if the expression is evaluated as **True**. Additionally, the optional **else** keyword can be used to execute another code when the statement is **False**. The overall format is shown below.

```
if EXPRESSION:
   # Code executed if True
   # More code executed if True
else:
# Code executed if False
```

The example shows the overall syntax of the **if** and **else** statements. Here, we can see an important aspect of the Python programming language: **Indentation**.

§ Indentation

Indentation describes the spaces between the left margin and the start of the text. In Python, indentation means that the code belongs to a **block of code.** In other words, it indicates whether a line is in the same block or not. Commonly, 2 or 4 *white spaces* or 1 *tab* can be used for indentation. However, it is highly recommended that only one kind should be used throughout the code, either whitespaces or tabs.

§ Multiple Conditions

Sometimes, we need to test various conditions. For this, we can have multiple **if...else** statements. Additionally, a shorter term for **else if** statements can be used: **elif**.

Example 1 – Multiple Conditions	Example 2 – Multiple Conditions
``# Multiple Conditions
a = 5
if a > 3:
# Code executed if a > 3
print("a > 3")
else if a < 3:
# Code executed if a < 3
print("a < 3")
else if a ==3:
# Code executed if a == 3
print("a = 3")```	```# Equivalent Example with elif
a = 5
if a > 3:
# Code executed if a > 3
print("a > 3")
elif a < 3:
# Code executed if a < 3
print("a < 3")
elif a == 3:
# Code executed if a == 3
print("a = 3")```
OUTPUT	OUTPUT
a > 3	a > 3

Here, we used the **print** function to show the results. In the next chapter, we will discuss its usage in more detail.

> **Further Readings – Print Function**
>
> The print function is used to show a representation of a Python object. More details are available on <u>Python official</u> <u>documentation</u>.

§ Nested Statements

In order to test multiple dependent conditions, if statements can be nested together, resulting in various blocks of code.

Example 1 – Nested Conditions	Example 2 – Nested Conditions
| ```python
a, b = 5, 2
if a > 2:
  # Code executed if a > 2
if b < 3:
  # Code executed if a>2 and b<3
    print("a > 2 and b < 3")
    if b == 2:
      # execute if a>2, b<3 and b=2
print(b)
``` | ```python
a, b = 5, 2
if a > 2 and b < 3:
  # Code executed if a>2 and b<3
  print("a > 2 and b < 3")
  if b == 2:
    # execute if a>2, b<3 and b=2
print(b)
``` |
| **OUTPUT** | **OUTPUT** |
| ```
a > 2 and b < 3
2
``` | ```
a > 3
2
``` |

3.6. Loops

There are two basic loops in Python, **for** and **while**. Both are used to loop through a block of code but have different use-cases.

3.6.1. While

The **while** loop repeats a block of code while a given expression is evaluated as True. The condition is tested before each execution.

```
while EXPRESSION:
    # Code executed while True
    # More code executed while True
```

Since evaluation occurs before the block execution, the block might not even run. Notice the presence of **indentation** for the block of code.

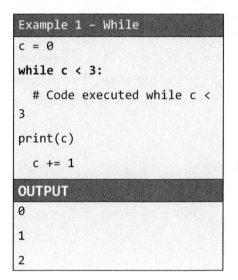

```
Example 1 - While
c = 0
while c < 3:
    # Code executed while c < 3
    print(c)
    c += 1
```
OUTPUT
```
0
1
2
```

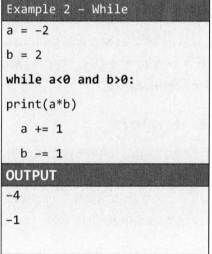

```
Example 2 - While
a = -2
b = 2
while a<0 and b>0:
    print(a*b)
    a += 1
    b -= 1
```
OUTPUT
```
-4
-1
```

In the examples above, it's obvious how *while* loop works. After each code block execution, the expression is re-evaluated to check if the block will be re-run again.

3.6.2. For

When you need finer control of the total number of executions, the **for** loop is used. In Python, **for loop** uses a sequence of elements defined as an **iterator**. The **for** loop iterates over each value in this sequence.

```
for VALUE in ITERATOR:
   # Code block
# More code executed
```

During each pass through the loop, a new value from the sequence is passed to the variable **VALUE**, until the sequence end is reached. Pay attention to the use of the **in** keyword before the operator.

OBS$_1$.: As in any other programming language, it is highly discouraged to modify the iterating object during the loop, since this can easily cause undesired behavior.

OBS$_2$.: The in keyword is also used to see if a value is present in a sequence (list, tuple, string, ...). In this case, it returns a Boolean value.

§ Iterators

Simply put, an **iterator** corresponds to a sequence of elements. In Python, **lists**, **tuples,** and **strings** are examples of iterable objects. If you want to create a sequence of integers to iterate over, the **range** function can be used.

The examples below show different kinds of iterators being used in **for** loops.

INPUT	INPUT
# FOR example 1	# FOR example 2
l = ["a", "b", "c"] # or tuple	s = "hi"
for i in l:	for c in s:
print(i)	print(c)

OUTPUT	OUTPUT
a	
b	h
c	i

§ Range **Function**

This built-in function creates a sequence of integers. It can be used with 1, 2, or 3 arguments. With one argument, the sequence starts from 0 until the given argument (excluded) with step unitary. Using with two arguments, the first corresponds to the initial (included) value or the sequence and the second to the final (excluded) value. Finally, with three arguments, it is like with two, but the third argument corresponds to the increment size. Check the examples below.

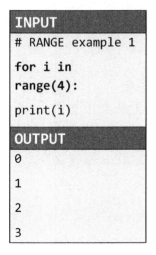
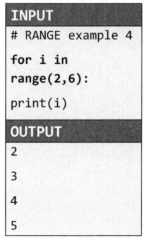
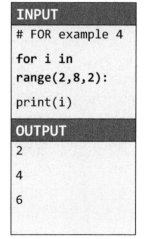

INPUT	INPUT	INPUT
# RANGE example 1	# RANGE example 4	# FOR example 4
for i in range(4):	for i in range(2,6):	for i in range(2,8,2):
print(i)	print(i)	print(i)

OUTPUT	OUTPUT	OUTPUT
0	2	2
1	3	4
2	4	6
3	5	

The examples show the usage of the range function and in the **for** loop. By now, you could have noticed that the **range** function could be used to generate the index for elements in lists. Indeed, this could be done, but using the sequence directly would be a more "Pythonic" approach. The example below illustrates this case.

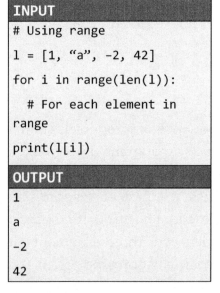

As you can see, the range function can be used to generate the index of each element in a list, but looping using the sequence directly is a more simple and understandable code.

Further Readings – Python

More details are available on Python official documentation. Get used to search and read this documentation. It is a great resource of knowledge.

3.7. Extra – Zen of Python

As a small Easter egg, Python has a collection of guiding principles for writing computer programs. You can check this by running the command below in the Python REPL.

```
>>> import this
```

After running the command, a text from <u>Tim Peters</u> will be printed. It shows the principles that were considered in the design of Python as a programming language.

```
The Zen of Python, by Tim Peters

Beautiful is better than ugly.
Explicit is better than implicit.
Simple is better than complex.
Complex is better than complicated.
Flat is better than nested.
Sparse is better than dense.
Readability counts.
Special cases aren't special enough to break the rules.
Even though practicality beats purity.
Errors should never pass silently.
Unless explicitly silenced.
In the face of ambiguity, refuse the desire to guess.
There should be one -- and preferably only one -- evident
way to do it.
Although that way may not be obvious at first excepting that
you're Dutch.
Now is better than never.
Although never is often better than *right* now.
If the implementation is tough to explain, it's a bad idea.
If the implementation is easy to explain, it may be a good
idea.
Namespaces are one honking great idea -- let's do more of
those!
```

Even though this is an Easter egg, all these tips are valuable, and any programmer should keep them in mind when creating new projects.

> ### Hands-on Time – Exercise
>
> Now, it is your turn. Follow the instructions in **the exercise below** to check your understanding of the basic syntax and structures of the language.

Exercise

Answer the questions below, then check your responses using the **Python REPL**.

1. **What's the type of each of these expressions?**

   ```
   >>> 1e-3
   ```

   ```
   >>> 2
   ```

   ```
   >>> 3.
   ```

   ```
   >>> 5 > 2
   ```

2. **The string definitions below are valid? Mark as True or False.**

   ```
   >>> "String\'s"          (    )
   ```

   ```
   >>> "HelloWorld'         (    )
   ```

   ```
   >>> 'This is a "quote"'   (    )
   ```

   ```
   >>> 'That's fine!'        (    )
   ```

3. **What are the results of the operations?**

   ```
   >>> -3 * 1
   ```

   ```
   >>> 5 % 3
   ```

   ```
   >>> 2 + 3 * 3
   ```

   ```
   >>> 1e1 + 1.5
   ```

   ```
   >>> True + 3
   ```

   ```
   >>> 3 ** False
   ```

```
>>> type(3 / 3)
>>> type(3. + 2)
>>> type(False + True)
>>> '123' * 2
>>> 'Hello' + "World"
>>> 2 - 2 / 4
>>> (2 - 2) / 4
>>> -1e1 + 8 // (1. + 1)
>>> 2 ** 2 ** 4
>>> 3 ** False
>>> 3 % 5 + (2 ** (6 / 3))
```

4. **What are the results of the sequence of commands?**

```
>>> a = b = 3
>>> c, d = 1, 2
>>> a + c == d * b - 2


>>> s = "a"
>>> s *= 3
>>> s + "b"


>>> a = 0
>>> a != 0 and True
```

```
>>> b = c = 42
>>> b /= 2
>>> b != 21 or c/b == 2


>>> b = False
>>> c = not b
>>> ((not c) and b) or True


>>> a = [1]
>>> a * 11


>>> a = [1, 2]
>>> b = [3, 4]
>>> a + b
```

5. **Consider the list li = [42, 1, 2, 3, 'A', 'B'], what the result of each alternative?**

a) >>> li[3]

b) >>> li[-2]

c) >>> li[:-3]

d) >>> li[-5:]

6. Which of the alternatives throws an error when executed?

```
>>> a = (1,2,3)
>>> a[3]
```

```
>>> b = [5, 6, 7, 8]
>>> b[-5]
```

```
>>> a = (1, 2)
>>> b = (3, 4)
>>> c = a / b
```

```
>>> a = (1,2,3)
>>> b = (1,2,3)
>>> a + b
```

```
>>> a = (1,2,3)
>>> b = (1,2,3)
>>> a * b
```

7. Write a script to solve the problem: consider a list of size n; if n is odd, the script shows the value in the middle of the list, if n is even, it shows the two values at the center of the list.

Examples:

list1 = [1,5,11,12,16] –> 11

list2 = [1,5,11,12] –> [5, 11]

Python for Data Analysis - Advanced

This chapter explores deeper concepts of Python, from a more advanced loop controls to handling text files. This chapter will also teach how to create functions, classes and new types of containers available in python.

4.1. Advanced Loops Concepts

Python has some syntaxes and definitions that extrapolate the concepts presented in the previous chapter.

4.1.1. Loop Control

Loops are used to control the flow of the program being written. Multiple times, you want to leave a loop earlier or test something after its end. Python has some keywords to be used for these specific cases: **break**, **continue,** and **else**.

§ Break

The break is used to leave the innermost loop statement. Primarily, it is used in conjunction with an **if** statement that looks to a specific condition to leave the loop.

EXAMPLE 1 - WHILE	EXAMPLE 2 - FOR
```# Print all values until``` `c=2` `while True:` `  if c == 2:` `    break` `  c += 1` `print(c)`	```# Print if find white space``` `m = "abc def"` `for c in m:` `  if c == " ":` `    print("White space found!«)` `    break`
OUTPUT	OUTPUT
1 2	White space found!

The capabilities of **break** are clear in the examples above. In the first example, the **while** loop would continue indefinitely, if it had not been for the conditional statement with the break keyword. The second example, prints "White space found!" and leaves the loop if the initial string contains a white space in its definition.

§ Continue

The **continue** statement ignores all the remaining lines of code in the block and continues to the next iteration of the innermost loop. This behavior is useful when you want to *ignore* a loop iteration but still want to continue iterating.

```
EXAMPLE - WHILE
# Print all values in range(6), except 0 and 5
for n in range(6):
  if n == 1 or n == 5:
continue
  print(n)
```
```
OUTPUT
0
2
3
4
```

§ Else

The **else** keyword can also be used in loop. In **while** loops, it is executed when the expression is evaluated as **False**. In **for** loop, it is executed when the iterator end is reached.

```
EXAMPLE 1 - WHILE
# Add 2 and print final
value
c = 0
# Print when c >= 3
while c < 3:
  c += 2
  print("Add 2")
else:
  print(c)
```
```
OUTPUT
Add 2
Add 2
4
```

```
EXAMPLE 2 - FOR
# Square and print when done
s = [3, 5]
# Iterate until c = 1
for i in  s:
  print(i ** 2)
else:
  print("Iterator ended! ")
```
```
OUTPUT
9
25
Iterator ended!
```

OBS.: The else block is not executed if the loop is terminated by a break statement.

4.1.2. List Comprehension

Multiple times, it is common to perform an operation or apply a condition to a list and store the result in a new **list**. We have seen that by using loops and conditional statements, we are capable of achieving the desired result. However, Python has an elegant and fast way to perform this operation called **List Comprehension**. Consider the equivalent examples below that calculate the square of a list.

Example – No List Comprehension	Example 1 – List Comprehension
``# Square all values
li = [2, 5, 3, 7]
r = []
for i in li:
r.append(i ** 2)
print(r)```	```# Square all values
li = [2, 5, 3, 7]
r = [i ** 2 for i in li]
print(r)```
OUTPUT	OUTPUT
`[4, 25, 9, 49]`	`[4, 25, 9, 49]`

Example – No List Comprehension	Example 2 – List Comprehension
``# Filter values above 3
li = [2, 5, 3, 7]
r = []
for i in li:
if i > 3:
r.append(i)
print(r)```	```# Filter values above 3
li = [2, 5, 3, 7]
r = [i for i in li if i > 3]
print(r)```
OUTPUT	OUTPUT
`[5, 7]`	`[5, 7]`

The result of the **List Comprehension** is always a new list. Using this feature to create simple operations and filter make the code relatively easy to understand and increases the execution time. Although a large nested list comprehension with multiple conditional statements are possible, they are not recommended because the code readability is considerably reduced. Therefore, simple operations and filter are the perfect use cases of list comprehension.

> **Further Readings – Nested List Comprehension**
>
> List Comprehension is one of the unique features of Python that may confuse new users. Nested ones are particularly more troublesome, but the Official Docs have great usage examples.

4.2. Advanced Containers

After being presented by `list` and **tuple**, there are other containers highly useful in Python: **Sets** and **Dictionaries**. Both are powerful data types for storing a collection of elements.

4.2.1. Sets

The definition of sets can be borrowed the mathematics: "A set is a well-defined collection of distinct objects." In Python, sets are used to represent an unordered collection without duplicates. Therefore, they are used to test membership and remove duplicates. Simple set operations support: **union, intersection, difference,** and **symmetric difference**. Since a set is an unordered container, values cannot be accessed by indexing. Additionally, **Sets** have their own operations invoked by built-in functions. To define a set, you just need to write a sequence of comma-separated values between curly brackets.

§ Defining Sets

Curly brackets are used in sets definitions.

```
PYTHON REPL:
>>> a = set()              # Empty set
>>> b = {1, 2, 3, 4, 5, 6}  # Set with numeric values
>>> c = {42, "hi", True}    # Set with compound types
>>> {1, 2, 2, 2, 1}         # Duplicates are removed
{1, 2}
```

OBS$_1$.: Careful, empty curly brackets, "{}", does not create an empty set, it creates a dictionary.

OBS$_2$.: Remember that set is an unordered collection and, therefore, its values cannot be indexed.

§ Function set()

Like lists and tuples, you can also create sets from previous objects such as strings, lists, and tuples.

```
PYTHON REPL:
>>> s = «abibliophobia»           # String
>>> li = [2, 3, 5, 5, 5, 2, 3, 3]  # List
>>> tu = (0, 1, 1, 0, 1, 0, 0, 0)  # Tuple
>>> set(s)                        # Unique letters in
word
{'a', 'b', 'h', 'i', 'l', 'o', 'p'}
>>> set(li)                       # Unique elements of
li
{2, 3, 5}
>>> set(tu)                       # Unique elements of
tu
{0, 1}
```

§ Add or Remove

Adds or removes a value from the set.

```
PYTHON REPL:

>>> s= {2, 3, 5}
>>> s.add(1)            # Add value 1 to set
>>> s
{1, 2, 3, 5}
>>> s.add(3)            # Nothing happens, value already in
the set
>>> s
{1, 2, 3, 5}
>>> s.remove(3)         # Remove value 3
>>> s
{1, 2, 5}
```

§ Union

Returns new set resulting from the union of two sets.

```
PYTHON REPL:

>>> s1, s2 = {2, 3, 5}, {2, 4, 1, 6, 5}
>>> s1.union(s2)                        # Union of sets
{1, 2, 3, 4, 5, 6}
>>> s1 | s2                             # Equivalent
{1, 2, 3, 4, 5, 6}
```

§ Intersection

Returns new set resulting from the intersection of both sets.

```
PYTHON REPL:

>>> s1, s2 = {2, 3, 5}, {2, 4, 1, 6, 5}
>>> s1.intersaction(s2)                 # Intersection
of sets
{2, 5}
>>> s1 & s2                             # Equivalent
{2, 5}
```

§ Difference

Returns new set resulting from the difference of sets.

```
PYTHON REPL:
>>> s1, s2 = {2, 3, 5}, {2, 4, 1, 6, 5}
>>> s1.difference(s2)              # Difference s1 and  s2
{3}
>>> s1 - s2                        # Equivalent
{3}
>>> s2.difference(s1)             # Difference s2 and s1
{1, 4, 6}
>>> s2 - s1                        # Equivalent
{1, 4, 6}
```

§ Symmetric Difference

Returns new set resulting from the symmetric difference of sets. Basically, it returns all the elements that are in only one of the sets. It could be, though, as the difference of the union and intersection of the sets.

```
PYTHON REPL:
>>> s1, s2 = {2, 3, 5}, {2, 4, 1, 6, 5}
>>> s1.symmetric_difference(s2)  # Symmetric diff s1 and s2
{1, 3, 4, 5}
>>> s2 ^ s1                       # Equivalent
{1, 3, 4, 5}
```

§ Set Comprehension

Sets can also be used in a similar manner as a list comprehension.

```
EXAMPLE - Set Comprehension
# Set comprehension - Get all consonants of a word
sc = {x for x in «spatulate» if x not in «aeiou»}
print(sc)
OUTPUT
{'l', 'p', 's', 't'}
```

Remember, the **in** keyword is used to check if the value is present in the list. Therefore, in the example, only consonants are selected.

4.2.2. Dictionaries

Dictionaries are a powerful data type present in python. It can store indexed values like lists, but the indexes are not a range of integers. Instead, they are unique **keys**. Therefore, dictionaries are a set of **key:value** pairs. Like sets, dictionaries are not ordered. The keys can be any immutable objects such as strings, tuples, integers, or float numbers.

§ Defining Dictionaries

Curly brackets and colon are used in an explicit dictionary definition.

PYTHON REPL:

```
>>> a = {}                    # Empty dictionary
>>> a = dict()                # Empty dictionary
>>> b = {1: 1, 2: 2, 3:3}     # Explicit definitions
>>> c = {42:2, «hi»: 1}
>>> d = {«A»:[1,2,3], «B»: 2}
>>> e = dict(k1=1, k22)       # Considered as string keys
```

§ Assigning Values to Keys

After a dictionary is created, you can assign values indexing by keys.

PYTHON REPL:

```
>>> d = {}                    # Empty dict
>>> d["a"] = [1, 2]           # Assigning list to key "a"
>>> d[2] = "Hello"            # Assigning string to key 2
>>> d
{'a': [1, 2], 2: 'Hello'}
>>> d[2] = «123»              # Overriding value in key 2
>>> d
{'a': [1, 2], 2: '123'}
>>> d[«b»]                    # Access invalid key
KeyError: 'b'
```

§ Get Keys and Values

Dictionary has the built-in methods **keys** and **values** to achieve the current values stored.

PYTHON REPL:

```
>>> d = {'a': [1, 2], 2: '123'}    # Same of previous
example
>>> d.keys()                       # List current keys
dict_keys(['a', 2])
>>> d.values()                     # List current values
dict_values([[1, 2], '123'])
```

OBS.: Remember that dictionaries are not an ordered object. Therefore, do not expect order in its keys or values, even though they maintain the insertion order in the latest Python version.

Further Readings – Order in Python Dictionaries

From Python 3.7+, dictionaries maintain the insertion order. The announcement of this as a feature in the mail list is available here.

§ Dictionaries in Loops

In general, you want to know the **key:value** pairs on a dictionary when iterating. The **items** method returns both values when used in for loops.

```
INPUT
# Nested Conditions
d = dict(a=1, b=2, c=3)
for k, v in d.items():
print(k)
    print(v)
```
```
OUTPUT
a
1
b
2
c
3
```

§ Dictionary Comprehension

Dictionaries can be used as in list comprehension.

```
EXAMPLE - Dict Comprehension
# Dict of cubes(values) of number(key) 1 to 4
dc = {x: x ** 3 for x in range(1, 5) }
print(dc)
```
```
OUTPUT
{1: 1, 2: 8, 3: 27, 4: 64}
```

4.3. Functions

We already used multiple functions that are built in the Python programming language, such as **print**, **len**, or **type**. Generally, a function is defined to represent a set of instructions that will be repeatedly called. In order to achieve the desired task, a function may or may not need multiple inputs, called arguments.

```
EXAMPLE – Built-in Functions
a = [1, 2, 3]
s = len(a)       # variable a is the argument of function len
print(s)         # variable s is the argument of function
print
OUTPUT
3
```

Not all functions need an argument, for example, the built-in function **help**.

```
EXAMPLE – Built-in Functions
help()              # no values is passed as argument
OUTPUT
Welcome to Python 3.6's help utility!
...
```

Further Readings – Python Functions

As always, the Official Documentation is a great source of further reading and reference about functions in Python.

4.3.1. User-Defined Functions – UDF

A function can be created using the **def** keyword, followed by the parameters and colon. The overall function format is shown below.

```
def FUNCTION_NAME(P1, P2):
  # Code executed when function called
  return VALUE_RETURNED # Optional
```

The FUNCTION_NAME is a placeholder for the name of the function. P1 and P2 are called parameters. They represent values passed to function and are not mandatory. Additionally, if you want your function to return a value, you can use the **return** statement. To invoke a function, you type its name followed by arguments between parentheses, when applied.

Example 1 – Vowels in string	Example 2 – Count letter
| ```
def vowels(s):
    v = "aeiou"
    r = set()
    # For each character c
    for c in s:
        # Check if it is a vowel
        if c in v:
            r.add(c)
    return r
print(vowels("House"))
print(vowels("Potiguar"))
print(vowels("Abracadabra"))
``` | ```
def count_1(s):
    r = dict()
    # For each character c
    for c in s:
        # Check if in keys
        if c in r.keys():
            # Add 1 to value in key c
            r[c] += 1
        else:
            # creates the key c
            r[c] = 1
    return r
print(count_1("Hello"))
print(count_1("Bosses"))
``` |
| **OUTPUTS** | **OUTPUT** |
| {'u', 'o', 'e'}
{'a', 'i', 'o', 'u'}
{'a'} | {'H': 1, 'e': 1, 'l': 2, 'o': 1}
{'B': 1, 'o': 1, 's': 3, 'e': 1} |

In the first example, the function returns a set with all the vowels present in the string. Whereas in the second example, a dictionary with each letter and its occurrence is returned. With the functions defined, you can apply the same logic to different inputs.

OBS₁.: The variable "s" is called parameters, it is the name that we reference the arguments passed to the function. For example, in vowels **("House"), "House" is the parameters used that will be referred to as "s" inside the function.**

OBS₂.: Return statement is not mandatory. If omitted the functions returns None.

OBS₃.: Function execution is immediately stopped when the return statement is executed.

§ Function Docstrings

This is a way to describe the functionality of your function. It comes immediately after the colon in function definition, using text between triple """" or '''.

```
Example - Docstrings
def add(a,b):

"""""

This is a function doc string; it is where your function is
described.

e.g., This function adds a and b.

"""""

return a + b
```

§ Passing Arguments

When calling functions, there are two ways to pass arguments: positional arguments and keyword arguments. The first methods the order in which the arguments are present in definition of the function is followed. Whereas in the second manner, the order does not matter, but each argument should be passed together with its parameters in the format **parameter=argument.** Consider the function defined below and the examples.

Function Definition		
def test(a, b, c):		
print('Test Function')		
Example 1 – Positional	Example 2 – Keyword	Example 3 – Combined
test(1, 2, 3)	test(c=3, b=2, a=1)	test_args(1, 2, c=3)

All these function calls are equivalent, just the way the arguments that are passed are changing.

OBS.: When passing arguments, all positional arguments should be passed before keyword arguments.

§ Function Arguments

Python functions can have four types of arguments:

o **Required Arguments**: When the argument is mandatory to the execution of the function. If this argument is not passed an error is shown.

o **Default Arguments:** In this case, this function works even if the argument is not passed. When this occurs, a default value is used.

o **Keyword Arguments**: A way to pass arguments by the parameter name.

o **Variable Number of Arguments**: A function can have an unknown number of required arguments and keyword arguments. In this case, extra positional arguments are stored in the tuple **args** and extra keyword arguments in the dictionary **kwargs**. This must be specified during the function definition.

Consider the given function. The parameters *args and **kwargs work as a placeholder as extra positional and keyword arguments passed, respectively.

```
Function Definition
def sum_values(a, b, c=2, *args, **kwargs):
  # Required arguments
  result = a + b
  # Default argument
  result += c
  # Variable arguments
  for v in args:
    result += v
  # variable kw arguments
  for k, v in kwargs.items():
    result += v
  # Show extra positional and keyword args
  print(args)
  print(kwargs)
  return result
```

This function first adds the values of the required arguments **a** and **b**. It then adds the third default argument **c.** If **c** is not passed during the function call, its values will receive the default value 2. If more than three positional arguments are passed, the values are stored in the list **args** that are added too. Finally, extra keyword arguments are stored in the kwargs dictionary that is also added. The examples below represent many ways to call this function using all these kinds of arguments.

Example 1 – Only Positional	Example 2 – Keyword
# Values of a, b, and c	# c defaults to 2
sum_values(1, 2, 3)	sum_values(b=2, a=1)
OUTPUT	OUTPUT
()	()
{}	{}
6	5
Example 3 – Only Required	**Example 4 – Extra Positional**
# Required arguments	# Extra positional arguments
sum_values(1, 2)	sum_values(1, 2, 3, 4, 5, 6)
OUTPUT	OUTPUT
()	(4, 5, 6)
{}	{}
5	21

Example 5 – Combined	Example 6 – Combined
# Extra keyword arguments d and e	# Extra pos/kw arguments
sum_values(1, 2, c=5, d=1, e=4)	sum_values(1, 2, 3, 4, e=5, f=6)
OUTPUT	OUTPUT
()	(4,)
{'d': 1, 'e': 4}	{'e': 5, 'f': 6}
13	21

§ Unpacking Arguments

You can also use tuples and dictionaries to pass parameters to functions. A single asterisk is used to perform the unpacking for tuple (or list) and double for dictionaries.

Function Definition	
def test(a, b): print('Test Function')	
Example 1 - *args	Example 2 - **kwargs
t = (1, 2) # Same as test(1,2) test(*t)	d = {"a": 1, "b": 2} # Same as test(a=1, b=2) test(**d)
Example 3 - Combined	Example 4 - Combined
t = (1, 2) # Same as test(1, 2, 1, 2) test(1, 2, *t)	d = dict(f=1, g=2) # Same as test(1, b=2, f=1, g=2) test(1, b=2, **d)

§ Lambda Expressions

Lambda expressions are small anonymous functions. It is generally used to pass small functions as arguments. Its overall format is shown below.

```
lambda INPUTS: OUTPUTS
```

The result is a function. Therefore, it should only be applied where small functions are expected. For example, there is a function called **sorted**, which sorts the values on a list. **key** is one of the parameters of this function that accepts another function that will be used to sort values in the list.

Example - Lambda Expressions
obj = ["Apple", "Pen", "Wallet", "Camera", "Glass"] # Sort by last letter s = sorted(obj, key=**lambda x: x[-1]**) print(s)
OUTPUT
['Camera', 'Apple', 'Pen', 'Glass', 'Wallet']

In the example, a lambda function is passed to the **sorted** function. This function has the input x and outputs the last value of x. In this case, x are strings inside the list **obj**, and the outputs are the last letter of these strings. Then, we are sorting the initial list by the last letter of the strings. This is a perfect use case of lambda functions when you need a simple function to be passed as an argument.

4.4. Classes

As most of the other widely used programming languages, Python also supports object-oriented programming. It is a way to design computer programs made of interacting objects. In Python, classes are the recipe for object creation.

> **Further Readings – OOP**
>
> Object Oriented Programming is a huge field by itself. This free book presents most of the basics and general concepts about OOP. Additionally, to facilitate the understanding, all the examples utilized are in Python.

If this seems an abstract concept, do not worry. Most of the things we were handling so far are objects in Python. Here, we will learn how to create the instructions for the creation of objects, a **Class**.

Basically, classes are composed of two things:

- o **Attributes**: There are class and instance attributes. They are variables used to store data regarding the class or instance.

- o **Methods**: They are functions defined within the class. These functions are used to modify data in each instance of the class (object).

Multiple examples of methods were already presented. For example, in the dictionary chapter, the **.keys()**, **.values(),** and `.items()` are methods of the dictionary **class**. That means most data types in Python are classes themselves.

§ Creating Classes

Classes can be created using the **class** keyword, followed by a colon. Generally, the first method of a class is the **__init__** function. The overall format is shown below.

```
class CLASS_NAME:
  # Attributes and methods
__init__(self, P1, P2):
    # Init code
```

The **CLASS_NAME** is a placeholder for the name of the class, obviously. The **__init__** function is called every time a new object of this class is created. Therefore, the function is used to assign values to object attributes or to perform other operations needed during the creation of an object instance. P1 and P2 are parameters used to pass values to the object creation. Furthermore, the object instances attributes are saved using the **self** keyword.

```
Example - Simple Class
class Adams:

  def __init__(self, question):

    self.answer = 42

    self.question = question


  def m1(self):

    print('Method executed! ')


q = Adams('Question of Life, the Universe, and Everything?
')
print(q.answer)
q.m1()
```
```
OUTPUT
42

Method executed!
```

In the example above, the class **Adams** contains the rules to create the **q** object. First, the object is created passing the **question** parameters. Then, this argument is stored in the question instance attribute. Finally, the attribute **answer** is printed, and the method **m1** is executed.

§ Multiple Instances

You can create multiple instances of the same class, each with its own attributes. The **self** parameter refers to the current instance of the class. It is used to access variables and methods of the class within the class definition.

Example 1 - Multiple Instances

```python
class AddMultCalc:

  add_symbol = '+'

  mult_symbol = 'x'

  def __init__(self, a, b):

    self.a = a

    self.b = b

  def add(self):

    r = self.a + self.b

    print(str(self.a) + self.add_symbol + str(self.b) + «=»
+
        str(r))

  def mult(self):

    r = self.a * self.b

    print(str(self.a) + self.mult_symbol + str(self.b) +
«=» +
        str(r))


c1 = AddMultCalc(5, 11)

c1.add()

c2 = AddMultCalc(-2, 5)

c2.mult()
```

OUTPUT

```
5+11=16

-2x5=-10
```

In this case, **add_symbol** and **mult_symbol** are class attributes. It is shared between instances and useful when defining constants.

§ Changing Attributes

You can modify the attributes of already created instances. Consider the same class defined previously.

Example 2 - Modify Attributes: Instance
| ```
c3 = AddMultCalc(-1, 4)

c3.add()

c3.a = -4

c3.add()
``` |
| **OUTPUT** |
| ```
-1+4=3

-4+4=0
``` |

Additionally, class attributes can also be modified using the class name and attribute.

Example 3 - Modify Attributes: Classes
| ```
AddMultCalc.add_symbol = «#»

c3 = AddMultCalc(-1, 4)

c3.add()
``` |
| **OUTPUT** |
| ```
-1#4=3
``` |

4.5. Modules Advanced

Previously, we have seen that modules are **.py** files with python code in it that can be executed. However, the main objective of modules is to permit code reusability. You can import a module by the file name or import individual functions and classes. Briefly, Python packages are multiple modules combined to perform a given task.

Further Readings - Python Modules

Further reading of Python modules and how they are executed are available in the Python documentation. This documentation has great information about namespaces and compiled files.

We have already seen that modules can be executed as scripts. Now, we will learn that they can also be imported. Save the code below in a file called **module.py**.

```
Module - module.py
class ShowAddClass:
  def __init__(self, a, b):
    self.a = a
    self.b = b
  def add(self):
    print(self.a + self.b)

def vowels(s):
  v = "aeiou"
  r = set()
  # For each character c
  for c in s:
    # Check if it is a vowel
    if c in v:
      r.add(c)
return r
```

This module contains a class **ShowAddClass** and a function **vowels**. You can reuse this code in another model by importing it.

4.5.1. Importing Modules

Modules can import other modules with the **import** statement. If you are in the same folder that the **module.py** was saved, there are multiple ways to import this module and use the classes and function defined in it.

OBS.: Since packages are modules, importing packages are like importing modules.

§ Direct Import

When using this method, all classes and functions in the module will be available through the module **namespace**. In other words, the function and classes are available using the module name and the ".".

PYTHON REPL:

```
>>> import module
>>> module.vowels("Hello World!")
{'e', 'o'}
```

§ Partial Import

You can also import only specific functions/classes from the module. In this case, the import format is changed to **from MODULE_NAME import FUNCTION/CLASS_NAME**. No additional namespace is created to invoke the function/class.

PYTHON REPL:

```
>>> from module import ShowAddClass
>>> s = ShowAddClass(2, 3)
>>> s.add()
5
```

You can use the *, to import all classes and functions available in the module without the namespace restriction.

PYTHON REPL:

```
>>> from module import *
>>> s = ShowAddClass(2, 3)
>>> s.add()
5
>>> vowels(«Hello»)
{'e', 'o'}
```

§ Using Alias

An alias can be used when importing an entire module or specific functions. In general, this is done to avoid namespace conflicts or reduce the module namespace length. The alias is created with the keyword **as**.

PYTHON REPL:

```
>>> import module as m
>>> s = m.ShowAddClass(1, -1)
>>> s.add()
0
```

In this example, the alias is used to avoid conflict with the variable vowels.

PYTHON REPL:

```
>>> vowels = "aeiou"
>>> from module import vowels as fun_vowels
>>> fun_vowels(vowels)
{'a', 'e', 'i', 'o', 'u'}
```

4.5.2. Executing Modules as Scripts

Writing classes and functions are preferred methods to create programs following OOP criteria. In Python, modules can also be executed as scripts and arguments passed to the module execution. Add the code below to the end of **module.py**.

```
if __name__ == «__main__»:
    import sys
    v = vowels(sys.argv[1])
print(v)
```

This code checks whether our module if being executed and is the **sys** built-in library to read the arguments script arguments and pass it to **vowels** function. Then, it prints the result. Running the command below results in the module execution.

```
python module.py test
{'e'}
```

Generally, the execution of modules is used to provide an interface to the module or to perform tests in the code.

Hands-on Time – Exercise

Now, it is your turn. Follow the instructions in the **Python_Advanced.pdf** file to check your understanding of the basic syntax and structures of the language.

Exercises

Answer the questions below. Then check your responses using the **Python REPL or creating and executing a .py file.**

1. **Check all options that contain keywords used in loop control?**

   break   (   )

   stop   (   )

   else   (   )

   continue   (   )

   in   (   )

2. **What command should be used to exit this while loop?**

```
while True:
    print("Hi")
```

   break

   stop

   terminate

   continue

3. **What's the output of the example below?**

```
i = 1
while True:
    print(i)
    i += 1
    if i == 42:
        break

print(i)
```

   40

   41

42

43

4. What's the output of the example below?

```
s = "acbdefgh"
m = ""
for c in s:
  if c in "aeiou":
    continue
  m += c
print(m)
```

abcdefgh

ae

cbdfgh

fgh

5. What's the output of the example below?

```
c = 0
while c < 1:
  c += 1
  print(c)
  if c == 1:
    break
else:
  print("Else executed!")
```

1

1

　Else executed

Else executed

Nothing is printed

6. What's the output of the example below?

```
i = []
for v in i:
  print("Iterating...")
else:
  print("Iteration over!")
```

Iterating...

    Iteration over!

Iterating...

Iteration over!

Nothing is printed

7. Are the lists comprehensions defined below valid? Mark as True or False.

```
lc = [a for b in range(5)]                    (    )
lc = [a for a in range(5) if a < 2]           (    )
lc = [b**2 for b in range(3)]                 (    )
lc = [[(a, b) for a in range(5)] for b in range(3)]
                                              (    )
```

8. What is the equivalent of this for loop as a list comprehension?

```
sqrt = []
for v in range(5, 10):
  sqrt.append(v ** .5)
```

sqrt = [v ** .5 for v in range(5)]

sqrt = [v ** 2 for v in range(5, 10)]

sqrt = [c ** .5 for v in range(5)]

sqrt = [v ** .5 for v in range(5, 10)]

9. **What is the equivalent of this for loop as a dict comprehension?**

```
dc = {}
for c in (1, 2, 3, 4, 5):
  dc[c] = c ** 2
```

dc = {c: c ** 2 for c in range(5)}

dc = {c: c ** .5 for c in range(1, 6)}

dc = {c: c ** 2 for c in range(1, 5)}

dc = {c: c ** 2 for c in range(1, 6)}

10. **What is the equivalent of this for loop as a set comprehension?**

```
sc = {}
for c in "abracadabra":
  if c != "a":
    sc.add(c)
```

sc = [c for c in "abracadabra"]

sc = [c for c in "abracadabra" if c == "a"]

sc = [c for c in "abracadabra" if c != "a"]

sc = [c for c in "brcdbrf"]

11. **Consider the sets defined below. What are the results of the operations?**

```
s1 = {1, 2, "B", 4, 5}
s2 = {1, "A", "B", "C", 5}
```

>>> s1 & s2

>>> s1 ^ s2

>>> s2 | s2

>>> s1 - s2

>>> s2 - s1

```
>>> s2 & s1
>>> s2 ^ s1
```

12. Given the function definition, what are the results of the function calls below?

```
def mult_values(a, b, c=.5, *args, **kwargs):
    result = a * b
    result *= c
    for v in args:
        result *= v
    for k, v in kwargs.items():
        result *= v
    print(args)
    print(kwargs)
    return result
```

a) `>>> mult_values(1, 2, d=2)`

   `>>> mult_values(b=2, a=1, d=1, f=2)`

   `>>> mult_values(1, 2, 3, 2, 2)`

b) `>>> mult_values(1, 2, 3, 2, 2, house=2)`

c) `>>> mult_values(1, 2, 1, 1, hi=2, hello=2, greetings=1)`

d) `>>> a = [1, 2, 3, 4, 5]`

   `>>> mult_values(*a)`

e) `>>> d = {"a":1, "b":2, "d":3}`

   `>>> mult_values(**d)`

f) `>>> d = dict(j=1, k=2)`

   `>>> a = [1, 2, 3, 4]`

   `>>> mult_values(1, 2, *a, **d)`

13. Are the Lambda Expressions defined below valid? Mark as True or False.

```
lambda x ** 2: x                                    (     )

x lambda : x ** 2                                   (     )

lambda b: b + 1                                     (     )

lambda x: x **2                                     (     )

lambda a: b ** 2                                    (     )
```

14. Given the class definition, what are the results of the alternatives below?

```
class Circle:
  pi = 3.14
  def __init__(self, radius):
    self.radius = radius

  def area(self):
    a = self.pi * r ** 2
    print('Area:' + str(a))

  def circumference(self):
    c = self.pi * r * 2
    print(' Circumference:' + str(c))
```

a)   >>> c = Circle(2)

        >>> print(c.radius)

b)   >>> c = Circle(2)

        >>> c.radius = 3

        >>> print(c.radius)

c)
```
>>> c = Circle((1/3.14)**2)
>>> c.area()
```

d)
```
>>> c = Circle(1/3.14)
>>> c.circumference()
```

e)
```
>>> c1 = Circle(1)
>>> c2 = Circle(2)
>>> c1.radius * c2.radius
```

f)
```
>>> c1 = Circle(1)
>>> c2 = Circle(2)
>>> c1.pi / c2.pi
```

g)
```
>>> Circle.pi = 1
>>> c = Circle(2)
>>> c.area()
```

15. Consider the generic module.py below. Which of the alternatives are valid import statements? Mark as True or False.

```
class Circle:
  pi = 3.14
  def __init__(self, radius):
    self.radius = radius

  def area(self):
    a = self.pi * r ** 2
    print('Area:' + str(a))

  def circumference(self):
    c = self.pi * r * 2
    print(' Circumference:' + str(c))

def add_area(c1, c2)
  return c1.area() + c2.area()


if __name__ == «__main__»:
    c = Circle(1/3.14)
    c.area()
```

```
import module.py                          (    )
in module import Circle                   (    )
from module import add_area               (    )
from module import *                      (    )
import module as c                        (    )
from module Circle as C                   (    )
from module import Circle as C            (    )
```

**16. What is printed when the module in the previous question
is executed?**

5

IPython and
Jupyter Notebooks

IPython and Jupyter Notebooks are two great tools capable of interactive computing and rich media output. Combined, they offer a great skill set for a Data Scientist. Let's dive into the details about each of these.

5.1. IPython

IPython, also known as Interactive Python, is a capable toolkit that allows you to experience Python interactively. It has two main components: an interactive Python Shell interface and Jupyter kernels.

These components have many features, such as:

- Persistent input history
- Caching of outputs
- Code completion
- Support for 'magic' commands
- Highly customizable settings
- Syntax highlighting

- Session logging
- Access to system Shell
- Support for Python's debugger and profiler

Now, let's explore each of these components and see how these features come to life.

5.2. Installing IPython

Using **pip,** run the command:

```
pip install ipython
```

With conda, just type:

```
conda install ipython
```

5.3. IPython Shell

The objective of this Shell is to provide a superior experience than the default Python REPL.

To run the IPython Shell, you simply need to call the command below on your system console.

```
ipython
```

§ Interface

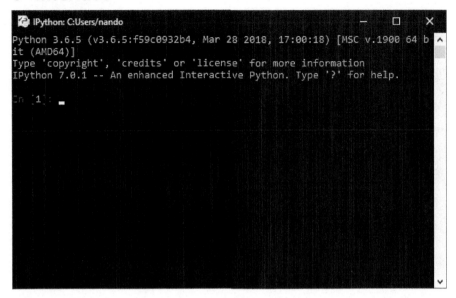

At first glance, the IPython Shell looks like a normal boring Shell, with some initial version information and some user tips. However, it has great features that make it shine.

§ Help

```
IPython: C:Users/nando                                    —    □    X
Python 3.6.5 (v3.6.5:f59c0932b4, Mar 28 2018, 17:00:18) [MSC v.1900 64 bit (AMD64)]
Type 'copyright', 'credits' or 'license' for more information
IPython 7.0.1 -- An enhanced Interactive Python. Type '?' for help.

In [1]: a=1

In [2]: a?
Type:        int
String form: 1
Docstring:
int(x=0) -> integer
int(x, base=10) -> integer

Convert a number or string to an integer, or return 0 if no arguments
are given.  If x is a number, return x.__int__().  For floating point
numbers, this truncates towards zero.

If x is not a number or if base is given, then x must be a string,
bytes, or bytearray instance representing an integer literal in the
given base.  The literal can be preceded by '+' or '-' and be surrounded
by whitespace.  The base defaults to 10.  Valid bases are 0 and 2-36.
Base 0 means to interpret the base from the string as an integer literal.
>>> int('0b100', base=0)
4

In [3]:
```

You can type "?" after an accessible object at any time you want more details about it.

§ Code Completition

```
Python 3.6.5 (v3.6.5:f59c0932b4, Mar 28 2018, 17:00:18) [MSC v.1900 64 bit (AMD64)]
Type 'copyright', 'credits' or 'license' for more information
IPython 7.0.1 -- An enhanced Interactive Python. Type '?' for help.

In [1]: pr
        %precision %prun
        print      %%prun
        property
```

You can simply press the *TAB* key at any time to trigger the code completion.

§ Syntax Highlight

```
Python 3.6.5 (v3.6.5:f59c0932b4, Mar 28 2018, 17:00:18) [MSC v.1900 64 bit (AMD64)]
Type 'copyright', 'credits' or 'license' for more information
IPython 7.0.1 -- An enhanced Interactive Python. Type '?' for help.

In [1]: s=

In [2]: a = 42

In [3]: len(s)
     3  6

In [4]: for c in s:
   ...:     print(c)
s
t
r
i
n
g

In [5]:
```

The code is automatically highlighted depending on the variables and keywords you are using.

§ Run External Commands

```
Python 3.6.5 (v3.6.5:f59c0932b4, Mar 28 2018, 17:00:18) [MSC v.1900 64 bit (AMD64)]
Type 'copyright', 'credits' or 'license' for more information
IPython 7.0.1 -- An enhanced Interactive Python. Type '?' for help.

In [1]: !pip install numpy
Requirement already satisfied: numpy in c:\program files\python36\lib\site-packages (1.1
5.4)

In [2]: !cd
C:\Users\nando

In [3]:
```

External commands can be run directly using "!" at the beginning of the input.

§ Magic Commands

```
IPython 7.0.1 -- An enhanced Interactive Python. Type '?' for help.

In [1]: %time sum(range(100000))
Wall time: 15.6 ms
    1   4999950000

In [2]: %timeit sum(range(100000))
2.59 ms ± 135 µs per loop (mean ± std. dev. of 7 runs, 100 loops each)

In [3]: a = 100

In [4]: b =

In [5]: %pdb
Automatic pdb calling has been turned ON

In [6]: a+b
---------------------------------------------------------------------------
TypeError                                 Traceback (most recent call last)
<ipython-input-6-ca730b97bf8a> in <module>
----> 1 a+b

TypeError: unsupported operand type(s) for +: 'int' and 'str'
> <ipython-input-6-ca730b97bf8a>(1)<module>()
----> 1 a+b

ipdb>
```

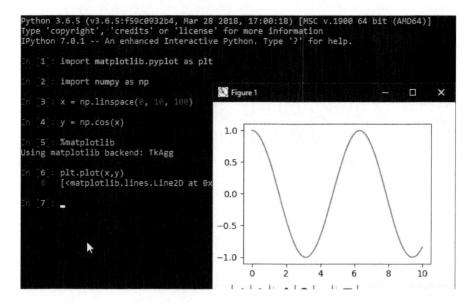

Magic commands add incredible capabilities to IPython. Some commands are shown below:

%time – Shows the time to execute the command.

%timeit – Shows the mean and standard deviation of the time to execute the command.

%pdb – Run the code in debug mode, creating breakpoints on uncaught exceptions.

%matplotlib – This command arranges all the setup needed for IPython to work correctly with Matplotlib. This way, IPython can display plots that are outputs of running code in new windows.

There are multiple magic commands that be used on IPython Shell. For a full list of the built-in commands, check this link or type "%lsmagic".

> ### Further Readings – IPython Shell
> If you are comfortable with reading documentations, feel free to go further and check their <u>documentation</u> for more information.

5.4. Jupyter Notebooks

The Jupyter Notebook is an incredible browser-based tool used to combine code, text, mathematics, graphs, and media in general. It expands the usual console approach bringing a web-based application capable of developing, executing, and documenting the code.

To run a Jupyter Notebook, you simply need to call the command below on your system console.

```
jupyter notebook
```

After running this command, a new window will pop up on your default browser with an interface. Let's explore it.

§ Dashboard

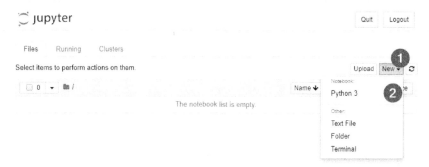

This is the Jupyter notebook Dashboard. It is where locally stored notebooks are displayed. It works like a file explorer. As you can see, there is no notebook. Let's change it by creating a new one by clicking on **New->Notebook: Python 3**, as shown.

§ Notebook Editor

Now, you are ready to edit your own notebook. But first, let's be familiar with the interface items listed above.

1. This is the notebook Cell. It is the simplest component of a notebook.

2. This drop-down menu alternates the kind of the selected cell. Each cell can have one of three types: Code, Markdown, and Raw.

3. This is the button that adds more cells to the notebook.

4. This button executes the current cells and selects the next one.

Ok, after this brief description of the main interface elements, you can start creating your notebook.

§ Cell Basics

Any of the three types of cells have two possible modes, **Command** and **Edit**.

Command Mode: The cell left edge is blue, and typing will send commands to the notebook. If in edit mode, you can change to command mode with the "ESC" key.

Edit Mode: The cell left edge is green, and there is a small grey pencil (✐) in the top right corner. Typing in this mode will edit the content of the cell. This mode can be achieved by double-clicking a markdown cell or single-clicking a code/raw cell. If you are in the *command mode*, you can change to *edit mode* with the *Enter* key.

```
In [ ]:
```

Running: Any cell can be executed using the interface button or the shortcuts:

"Ctrl+Enter": Run the current cell.

"Shift+Enter": Run the current cell and move to the next one.

Code Cells: Code cells can execute Python code. Any code not assigned to a variable will be shown as the output of the cell. Code cells have a "In []" on its left, indicating that it is an input cell, and the number inside the bracket reveals the order of execution.

```
In [1]:  a = 2 * 21

In [2]:  2 * 21
Out[2]:  42
```

Markdown Cells: This is how text can be added to the notebook. Markdown is a popular markup language that adds formatting to the text when rendered. The markdown language is only rendered after the cell execution, but in *edit mode*, the cell highlights the modifications that will be performed during rendering.

This markdown is not rendered
Therefore, its `markup` is not **fully** *shown*.
$$\int{e^x \cos(x)} dx$$

Hands-on Time – Markdown

A notebook explaining all the basic concepts of markdown is provided. Follow the notebook to understand the Markdown language.

Markdown_QuickGuide.ipynb.

§ Rich Media Output

One of the greatest advantages of Jupyter Notebooks is its capability of representing media. Code cells have built-in integration with Matplotlib graphs and many other kinds of media.

Matplotlib Plots: Any Matplotlib plot shown during a cell execution will be displayed in the cell output.

```
In [1]:  import matplotlib.pyplot as plt
         import numpy as np
```

```
In [2]:  x = np.linspace(0, 5, 100)
         y = np.cos(x)
         plt.plot(x,y)
```

Out[2]: [<matplotlib.lines.Line2D at 0x1a361fbd588>]

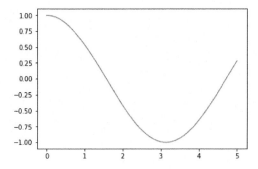

Audio Clips: Audio media can be displayed.

```
In [1]: import IPython.display as ipd
        ipd.Audio("https://www.soundjay.com/nature/rain-03.mp3")

Out[1]:
        ▶  0:00 / 0:30  ●━━━━  ◀))  ⋮
```

Video Clips: Video media can also be easily shown.

```
In [1]: import IPython.display as ipd
        ipd.Video("https://gcs-vimeo.akamaized.net/exp=1552672513~acl=%2A%2F402491449.mp
        ◀ ▓▓▓▓▓▓▓▓▓▓▓▓▓▓▓▓▓▓▓▓▓▓                                    ▶
```

Out[1]:

Tables: Tabular data visualization.

```
In [2]: import seaborn as sns

        iris = sns.load_dataset('iris')
        iris.head()
```

Out[2]:

	sepal_length	sepal_width	petal_length	petal_width	species
0	5.1	3.5	1.4	0.2	setosa
1	4.9	3.0	1.4	0.2	setosa
2	4.7	3.2	1.3	0.2	setosa
3	4.6	3.1	1.5	0.2	setosa
4	5.0	3.6	1.4	0.2	setosa

Further Readings – Display Module

With the capabilities of Jupyter notebooks, there are plenty of media files supported for display. For further reading, read the IPython Display Module Docs.

Hands-on Time – Jupyter Notebooks

A notebook reviewing all the basic concepts of Jupyter notebooks, as well as some tips and tricks, is provided. Go through the notebook to train your understanding.

Notebook_QuickGuide.ipynb

Numpy for Numerical Data Processing

In this chapter, we will explore a fundamental package for data analysis: Numpy. It has powerful multi-dimensional array capabilities with fast high-level mathematical operations and handy functions. When explaining concepts in multi-dimensional arrays, we will focus first on one dimension to easily create the generalization for the concept.

6.1. Numpy

Numpy is one of the most famous and widely used Python packages for efficient data processing. Its main object is the multi-dimensional array: **ndarray**. Some algorithms can have a considerable performance increase using the array class offered by the numpy library. Additionally, the Scipy ecosystem of software is built on top of this to provide various scientific and engineering methods.

6.2. Installing IPython

Using pip, run the command:

```
pip install numpy
```

With conda, just type:

```
conda install numpy
```

Generally, numpy is imported using the short **np** as an alias:

```
import numpy as np
```

6.3. Object ndarray

This is the main object implemented by the numpy package. Simply put, it is a multi-dimensional ordered container object. However, differently from Python's built-in list, Numpy arrays are homogeneous, i.e., all elements should be the same type.

> **Hands-on Time – Using IPython Shell**
>
> Now that we know the advantages of using **IPython Shell**, let's use it to check the examples provided. The syntax highlights and auto completion certainly make it a better alternative to the standard Python REPL.

6.3.1. Creating and Modifying Arrays

An array can be created using any array-like ordered objects in Python, such as lists or tuples. In order to create an array, the function **np.array()** is called with the list object. The type can be inferred from the data or given as an argument.

§ One-dimensional Arrays

The type is given to the **np.array()** command with the **dtype** keyword. Additionally, the type and dimension of the created array can be checked using the **dtype** and **ndim** class attributes, respectively.

IPYTHON SHELL:

```
>>> import numpy as np          # Numpy with its common alias

>>> a = np.array([1, 2, 3, 4]) # Create an array from a list
>>> a
array([1, 2, 3, 4])            # Int type inferred
>>> a.dtype
dtype('int32')                 # 1 dim array - list of values
>>> a.ndim
1


>>> b = np.array(42, dtype=float) # Create a float array
array(42.)
>>> b.dtype
dtype('float64')               # Float type given
>>> b.ndim
0                              # 0 dim array - single value
```

OBS$_1$.: From now on, we will assume that Numpy is imported as the alias np in all the IPYTHON SHELL examples.

OBS$_2$.: Notice that a single value can be considered an array with dimension 0.

§ Multi-Dimensional Arrays

Nested and array-like objects are used to construct the dimensions of the array. You can think of a multi-dimensional array as a set of arrays in the previous dimension. For instance, we have seen that 0-dimensional array corresponds to a single value, then a 1-dimensional array is a set of 0-dimensional arrays. And a 2-dimensional array is a set of 1-dimensional arrays and so on. This concept is illustrated in the table below.

Illustration	Dimensions	Description
	O	Single value
	1	Multiple single values (List)
	2	Multiple List of values (Matrix)
	3	Multiple Matrices of values (Cube)
	4	Collection of Cubes
...	...	...

The same logic follows for more than 3 dimensions. You can think of a 4-dimensional array as a collection of Cubes arrays. However, beyond 3 dimensions, it is not easily illustratable and intuitive. The attributes **shape** and `size` are useful attributes for multi-dimensional arrays. The first returns the size of the array in each dimension, and the second returns the total number of elements present in the array.

```
IPYTHON SHELL:
```

```
>>> a = np.array([[1, 2, 1],   # Create an array from
                                 nested lists
               [3, 4, 3]])
>>> a
array([[1, 2, 1],
       [3, 4, 3]])
>>> a.ndim
2
>>> a.shape                    # Shape of the 2-dim array
(2, 3)
>>> a.size
6
>>> b = np.array(((1, 2),      # Create an array from
                                 nested tuples
                 (3, 4)),
                ((5, 6),
                 (7, 8))))
>>> b
array([[[1, 2],
        [3, 4]],
       [[5, 6],
        [7, 8]]])
>>> b.ndim
3
>>> b.shape                    # Shape of the 3-dim array
(2, 2, 2)
>>> b.size
8
>>> c = np.array([[1,2], [1]]) # Inconsistent number
                                 of columns
>>> c
array([list([1, 2]), list([1])], dtype=object)
```

OBS.: As shown in array c, be careful with the number of values in each dimension of the array. They should be consistent,

along with the definition. Otherwise, the dimension will be ignored, and you create an array of lists.

§ Creating Filled Arrays

In general, it is common to create arrays filled with a constant value or with a range of values. For that, there are five useful functions in Numpy: `np.zeros()`, `np.ones()`, `np.full()`, `np.linspace()`, and `np.arange()`. The examples illustrate the behavior of the functions.

```
IPYTHON SHELL:

>>> np.ones((2, 2))        # Array of 1s with shape (2,2)
array([[1., 1.],
       [1., 1.]])

>>> np.zeros((1, 2))       # Array of 0s with shape (2,2)
array([[0., 0.]])

>>> np.full((1, 3), -2)    # Array of -2 with shape (1, 3)
array([[-2, -2, -2]])

>>> np.linspace(0, 1, 3)   # Sequence of 3 elements
                           # between 0 and 1
array([0., 0.5, 1.])

>>> np.arange(0, 10, 5)    # Values from 0 to 10
                           # with step 5
array([0, 2, 4, 6, 8])
```

OBS.: Prefer to use `np.linspace()` **over** `np.arange()` **for arrays with float values to have predictable number of values.**

§ Reshaping Arrays

Created arrays can be reshaped with the **reshape** method. The only restriction is that the new format should have the same number values as the previous. If one dimension is set to −1, the dimension is inferred from the remaining. The method **ravel** returns a flattened view.

```
IPYTHON SHELL:
```

```
>>> r = np.arange(1, 10, 2)    # Values from 1 to 10
                               with step 2
>>> r.reshape((3, 2))          # Reshape to (3, 2)
array([[ 0,  2],
       [ 4,  6],
       [ 8, 10]])
>>> r.reshape((2, -1))             # Invalid shape
array([[ 0,  2,  4],
       [ 6,  8, 10]])

>>> r.reshape((2, 2))              # Invalid shape
ValueError: cannot reshape array of size 6 into shape (2,2)
>>> a.ravel()                      # Flattened array
array([ 0,  2,  4,  6,  8, 10])
```

§ Appending to Arrays

Differently of lists, numpy arrays have fixed sizes. Therefore, to append a value in the array, a new array is created, and the values are copied. This can be done with the **append** function, which accepts values or other arrays. For large arrays, this is a costly operation and should be avoided. A good practice is to create the array with extra spaces and fill it.

IPYTHON SHELL:

```
>>> ar = np.arange(5)              # Values from 0 to 5
                                   with step 1
>>> ar2 = np.append(ar, 5)         # New array with
                                   value appended
array([0, 1, 2, 3, 4, 5])

>>> ar3 = np.append(ar, [5, 6]) # New array with
                                   values appended
array([0, 1, 2, 3, 4, 5, 6])

>>> ar
array([0, 1, 2, 3, 4])
```

§ Stacking and Concatenating Arrays

There are several functions that can perform the combinations of arrays, such as **hstack** and **vstack**. These functions are easily understandable when applied to arrays up to three dimensions. For more dimensions, the general functions **stack** and **concatenate** are more appropriate.

```
IPYTHON SHELL:
>>> ar1 = np.zeros((2,2))        # 2x2 with 0s
>>> ar2 = np.ones((2,2))         # 2x2 with 1s
>>> np.vstack((ar1, ar2))        # Combine on first axis
array([[0., 0.],
       [0., 0.],
       [1., 1.],
       [1., 1.]])

>>> np.hstack((ar1, ar2))        # Combine on second axis
array([[0., 0., 1., 1.],
       [0., 0., 1., 1.]])

>>> np.concatenate((ar3, ar2), axis=1)
                                 # Equivalent to hstack
array([[1., 1., 0., 0.],
       [1., 1., 0., 0.]])

>>> ar4 = np.stack((ar2, ar1))   # Created new dimension
>>> ar4
array([[[1., 1.],
        [1., 1.]],

       [[0., 0.],
        [0., 0.]]])
>>> ar4.shape
(2, 2, 2)
```

6.3.2. Indexing, Slicing, and Iterating

The operation to access values or range of values from an array, as well as iterate over its values.

§ One-dimensional Arrays

The slicing, indexing, and iterating with one-dimensional arrays is equivalent to the same operation on normal Python lists. The same logic can be used to change values on the array.

```
IPYTHON SHELL:
>>> ar = np.lispace(0, 2, 6)   # Sequence from 0 to 2 with 6
values
>>> ar[3]                      # Indexing
1.5
>>> ar[0:2]                    # Slicing
array([0. , 0.5])
>>> ar[-1]                     # Indexing
2.0
>>> ar[-2] = 5                 # Modifying
>>> for i in ar:              # Iterating
>>>     print(i)
0.0
0.5
1.0
1.5
5.0
```

§ Multi-Dimensional Arrays

Indexing arrays with multiple dimensions are done with a tuple with a value for each dimension. However, if an index value is omitted, it is considered a complete slice, which is equivalent to ":". Additionally, the "..." can be used in the indexes to represent as many as ":" as needed. Iterating on a multi-dimensional array is always performed in the first dimension.

Numpy also has the capability to perform each element iteration with the **np.nditer** function, but this function treats the values as read-only by default. In general, it is easier and more intuitive to use the first dimension during iteration over the multi-dimensional array.

Further Readings – np.nditer

To read further about how nditer iterates over a Numpy array, follow the documentation link. Additionally, read the multiple parameters accepted by this function and how it relates to arrays in C or Fortran.

IPYTHON SHELL:

```
>>> mat = np.arange(9).reshape((3,3))
                        # 3x3 Matrix from 0 to 8
>>> mat
array([[0, 1, 2],
       [3, 4, 5],
       [6, 7, 8]])
>>> mat[1, 1]           # Indexing
4
>>> mat[1, :]           # Slicing
array([3, 4, 5])
>>> mat[1]              # Equivalent
array([3, 4, 5])

>>> mat[0, :]
array([6, 7, 8])
>>> mat[0, ...]         # Equivalent
array([6, 7, 8])

>>> for row in mat:     # Iterating on the first dimension
>>>     print(row)
[0 1 2]
[3 4 5]
[6 7 8]
>>> for row in mat:     # Iterating on the first dimension
>>>     print(row)
[0 1 2]
[3 4 5]
[6 7 8]
>>> for v in np.nditer(mat): # Iterating each value
>>>     print(v)
0
1
2
3
4
5
6
7
8
```

§ Boolean Indexing

Numpy array also allows Boolean indexing. True and False means if the value will be returned or not, respectively. You can use Boolean indexing to perform filter operations on arrays, such as get values above or below a given threshold. Additionally, multiple conditions can be performed at the same time and more advanced filters created with this type of indexing. This can simply be done by using comparison operations between arrays and values. The operators & (and) |(or) are used to combine multiple conditions between parentheses.

IPYTHON SHELL:

```
>>> mat = np.arange(9).reshape((3,3)) # 3x3 Matrix
                                        from 0 to 8
>>> index = mat > 3                    # Indexes
>>> index
array([[False, False, False],
       [False,  True,  True],
       [ True,  True,  True]])
>>> mat[index]                         # Only values above 3
array([4, 5, 6, 7, 8])
>>> mat[mat > 3]                       # Equivalent
array([3, 4, 5])
>>> mat[(mat>3) & (mat<6)]             # Multiple comparison
array([3, 4, 5])
>>> mat[(mat>3) | (mat<1)]             # Multiple comparison
array([0, 4, 5, 6, 7, 8])
```

This is the best way to filter specific values in a Numpy array.

6.4. Operations and Functions

Numpy arrays support arithmetic operations as expected. Here, we will see some caveats of Broadcasting and built-in functions of the arrays.

> **Hands-on Time – Using IPython Shell and .py**
>
> Keep using **IPython Shell** to check the examples below. This will help you to have more experience with the Numpy package. Additionally, you can also run the examples with **ipython script.py**.

6.4.1. Basic Operations

The same basic operations present in standard Python are also present in Numpy arrays. In this case, the operation between arrays of the same shape results in another array.

IPYTHON SHELL:

```
>>> a = np.array([1, 2, 3], dtype=float)
>>> b = np.array([-1, 1, 3], dtype=float)
>>> a + b                       # Addition
array([0., 3., 6.])
>>> a - b                       # Subtraction
array([2., 1., 0.])
>>> a * b                       # Multiplication
array([-1,  2,  9])
>>> a / b                       # Division
array([-1.,  2.,  1.])
>>> a//b                        # Integer division
array([-1.,  2.,  1.])
>>> a % b                       # Modulus
array([-0.,  0.,  0.])
>>> a ** b                      # Power
array([ 1.,  2., 27.])
```

6.4.2. Advanced Operations

There is also support for operations and transformations beyond the basics. Some advanced matrix operations are easily usable by functions in the **linalg** namespace, attributes, and methods of the object, for example, matrix product, determinant, inverse, etc.

IPYTHON SHELL:

```
>>> a = np.array([[1, 0], [2, -1]], dtype=float)
>>> b = np.array([[1, 1], [0, 1]], dtype=float)

>>> a @ b                    # Matrix product
array([[1., 1.],
       [2., 1.]])

>>> np.dot(a, b)             # Equivalent
array([[1., 1.],
       [2., 1.]])

>>> a.T                      # Tranpose
array([[ 1.,  2.],
       [ 0., -1.]])

>>> np.linalg.inv(b)         # Inverse
array([[ 1., -1.],
       [ 0.,  1.]])

>>> np.linalg.det(a)         # Determinant
-1.0
```

6.4.3. Broadcasting

Broadcasting is a great feature that allows great flexibility. Shortly, broadcasting is the ability to perform an operation between arrays that do not have the exact same size or shape. It is based on two rules:

1. **If an array has fewer dimensions, a '1' will be prepended to the shape of this array until both arrays have the same dimensions.**

2. **Arrays with size 1 in a specific dimension perform as if they had the same dimension of the array with the largest size in that dimension.**

Do not worry. These rules are not easily understandable when written, but they make perfect sense on examples. Additionally, broadcasting allows vectorized operations with high performance and memory efficiency. The name comes from the reality that the smaller array is *broadcasted* to fit the dimension of the larger one. Examples and detailed explanations are shown below:

Example 1	Example 2
```a = np.array([1., 0., -1., 2.])``` `b = a + 1` `c = a + np.ones(4)` `print(b)` `print(c)`	```a = np.array([[1., 0], [1, 1]])``` `b = a - 1` `c = a + np.full((2,2), -1)` `print(b)` `print(c)`
OUTPUTS	**OUTPUT**
`[2. 1. 0. 3.]` `[2. 1. 0. 3.]`	`[[ 0. -1.]` `[ 0.  0.]]` `[[ 0. -1.]` `[ 0.  0.]]`
Example 3	Example 4
```a = np.array([[1., 0.], [-1., 2.]])``` `b = np.array([3., 1.])` `c = a + b` `print(c)`	```a = np.arange(8).reshape(2,2,2)``` `b = np.ones((2,2))` `c = a + b` `print(c)`

```
OUTPUTS
[[4. 1.]
 [2. 3.]]
```

```
OUTPUT
[[[1. 2.]
  [3. 4.]]
 [[5. 6.]
  [7. 8.]]]
```

In **Example 1,** the first thing that happens is to fit the scalar value in the same dimension as the array a, resulting in an array **np.array([1])**. Then, since this dimension has size 1, it will be broadcasted to fit the size of the larger array, in this case, 4. As shown, that is equivalent to the operation executed in the array **c**.

While in **Example 2**, the scalar value is converted to the array **np.array([[-1]])**. After that, the dimensions with size 1 will be extended to fit the larger array. In this case, 2 for dimension 0 and 2 for dimension 1. Similarly, the array **c** presents the same result.

Examples 3 and **4** show similar behavior but with more dimension. First, the dimension is added to the array **b** to have the same dimension of **a**. Then, the array is repeated in this dimension to fit the larger array.

6.4.4. Built-in Functions

In addition to operations, arrays have multiple functions to facilitate descriptive statistics calculations. Additionally, the namespace random contains functions to create random variables in multiple different types of distributions. Now, we will be using the **randn**, which receives the size of the desired array sample from a normal distribution with mean 0 and standard deviation 1.

Further Readings – Random

The numpy.random namespace has multiple useful functions for sampling various statistical distributions. The documentation explores more descriptive examples for each function and method.

IPYTHON SHELL:

```
>>> np.random.seed(42)          # Replicability
>>> a = np.random.randn(50)     # 50 values from
                                  normal distribution
>>> a.mean()                    # Mean
-0.28385754369506705
>>> a.std()                     # Standard Deviation
0.8801815954843186
>>> a.max()                     # Max value
1.8522781845089378
>>> a.min()                     # Min value
-1.9596701238797756
>>> a.argmax()                  # Index of max value
22
>>> a.sum()                     # Sum of values
-14.192877184753353

>>> a.reshape((2, 25)).mean(axis=1) # Mean on axis 1
(lines)
array([-0.37612378, -0.19159131])
```

OBS$_1$: The seed function guarantees the replicability of the result. Otherwise, the results will change since the values are sampled from a random function.

OBS$_2$: For multi-dimensional arrays the functions can be applied in a specific dimension, with axis=0 being in the columns and axis=1 the rows. This is shown in the last example.

Hands-on Time – Exercise

Now, it is your turn. Follow the instructions in **Numpy_ Exercises.ipynb** file to check your understanding of the basic syntax and structures of the language.

7

Pandas for
Data Manipulation

It is finally time to start working with data directly. As a data analyst, you will need a powerful tool to manipulate, move, and process data in Python. In this chapter, we will explore another fundamental package called Pandas.

7.1. Pandas

Pandas provides fast, simple, and flexible functions and structures to manipulate data easily and intuitively. It is highly suited for tabular data that can be easily expressed on its fundamental data structures, Series, and DataFrame. Those structures are the base classes of the package, and through them, Pandas provides multiple functionalities:

- Handling missing data;
- Data insertion/deletion;
- Powerful grouping, indexing, and combining; and
- Easily handle external files.

Those capabilities make Pandas one of the most important frameworks for anyone working with data in Python.

Additionally, in the background, Pandas uses Numpy to perform highly optimized vectorized operations. Pandas is also part of the Scipy Ecosystem.

7.2. Installing Pandas

Using pip, run the command:

```
pip install pandas
```

With conda, just type:

```
conda install pandas
```

Generally, Pandas is imported using the short **pd** as an alias:

```
import pandas as pd
```

7.3. Basics Structures

Pandas data fundamental data structures are divided per dimension, Series for 1D data, and DataFrame for 2D data. We will examine each of these structures in detail.

7.3.1. Series

Series is the Pandas 1-dimensional structure. It is composed of two collections: index and the data itself. The index represents the label of the values in a Series. If not provided an integer, a continuous series is automatically created. You can think of a Series as a handy combination between a Numpy array and the assignment capabilities of a Python dictionary.

Hands-on Time – Using IPython Shell

Keep using the **IPython Shell**. Once again, we will use it to check the examples provided with all the features of this shell.

§ Creating Series

Multiple objects can be used to create a Series with the **pd.Series** function. But overall, the command usage is maintained. The index size should match the size of the data passed, and some Numpy array attributes are also present in the Series object. The Numpy array equivalent of the Series is available with the **values** attribute.

IPYTHON SHELL:

```
>>> import pandas as pd          # Pandas with its
                                   common alias

>>> a = pd.Series([1, 2, 3])     # Create a Series
                                   from a list
>>> a
array([1, 2, 3, 4])              # Int type inferred
0    1
1    2
2    3
dtype: int64
>>> a.ndim
1
>>> b = pd.Series({'a':1.5, 'b':1, 'c':0})
                                 # Using a dictionary
>>> b.dtype
dtype('float64')                # Float type
>>> b.values
array([1.5, 0. , 1. ])          # Equivalent numpy array

>>> c = pd.Series([4, 3, 2], index=range(2, 5))
                                 # Index and data
```

OBS.: In pandas, the index has no restriction of uniqueness during creation. If an operation that requires a unique index is attempted, an exception is thrown.

§ Similarity with Numpy Arrays

As seen previously, Series have multiple similarities with Numpy arrays. Beyond attributes, aggregation functions and indexing are also identical.

IPYTHON SHELL:

```
>>> import numpy as np
>>> d = pd.Series([-1, 2, np.nan, 4, 5])
>>> d.mean()                        # Mean method
0.0

>>> d[:2]                           # Slicing
0    -2.0
1    -1.0
dtype: float64

>>> d[d>1]                          # Boolean indexing
4    2.0
dtype: float64

>>> d + 1                           # Broadcasting
0    -1.0
1     0.0
2     NaN
3     2.0
4     3.0
dtype: float64

>>> d ** 2
0    4.0
1    1.0
2    NaN
3    1.0
4    4.0
dtype: float64
```

OBS.: As Numpy, Pandas supports np.nan as "Not a Number" value.

§ Similarity with Dictionaries

Values assignments in Series are like dictionaries. The index is the equivalent of the key, and you can check if a value is present or not in the index.

```
IPYTHON SHELL:

>>> e = pd.Series([42, 1, 0, -2], index= ['a', 'b', 'c', 'd'])
>>> e['b'] = 101.1              # Assigment
>>> e['b']
101.1

>>> 'c' in e                   # Check for value in index
True

>>> e.index                    # Index attribute
Index(['a', 'b', 'c', 'd'], dtype='object')

>>> e['g']                     # Exception of invalid key
KeyError: 'g'
```

§ Unique Features

Series also have some unique features that do not have a direct parallel from what has been seen. For instance, the **describe** method that returns multiple statistical information about the data, or even the method **isin** that checks if the values are in another list-like object. The attribute **name** can be used to briefly explain the data present in the Series, and you can change the **dtype** attribute with the **astype** method. These highly efficient methods are what make Pandas excel during data manipulation.

IPYTHON SHELL:

```
>>> f = pd.Series([np.nan, 2, 3, 5, 7, np.nan],
name='primes')
>>> f.describe()          # Statistical description
count    4.000000
mean     4.250000
std      2.217356
min      2.000000
25%      2.750000
50%      4.000000
75%      5.500000
max      7.000000
Name: primes, dtype: float64

>>> f.isin([1, 2, 3])   # New boolean Series in that values
0    False
1     True
2     True
3    False
4    False
5    False
Name: primes, dtype: bool

>>> f.rename('renamed_primes')  # New Series reanamed
0    NaN
1    2.0
2    3.0
3    5.0
4    7.0
5    NaN
Name: renamed_primes, dtype: float64
>>> f.astype('str')
0    nan
1    2.0
2    3.0
3    5.0
4    7.0
5    nan
Name: primes, dtype: object
```

OBS$_1$.: Most operations in Pandas return a new object by default. The reason is to maintain the history of the operations easily accessible.

OBS$_2$.: By default, describe statistics, ignores "NaN" values.

OBS$_3$.: In Pandas, string values are represented by object dtype.

§ Advanced Types

Beyond the basic Numpy **dtypes**, the Pandas Series supports highly useful ones such as **datetime**, **strings,** and **categorical**. After conversion, they can be easily accessed with the proper accessor: **dt**, **str,** and **cat**. Using these accessors, you can efficiently modify/identify the data in the series with built-in functions.

IPYTHON SHELL:

```
>>> g = pd.Series(['apple', 'pen', 'pen', 'apple', 'pen'],
name='fruits', dtype='category')
>>> g.cat.categories             # Access Categories
Index(['apple', 'pen', 'penaple'], dtype='object')

>>> h = pd.Series(['brasil', 'china', 'canada', 'germany'],
name='countries')                # str type inferred
>>> h.str.upper()                # Apply upper to all values
0      BRASIL
1       CHINA
2      CANADA
3     GERMANY
Name: countries, dtype: object

>>> i = pd.Series(['2019-01', '2019-02', '2019-03', '2019-
04'], name='dates')
>>> i = pd.to_datetime(i)        # Convert to datetime
>>> i.dt.year
0      2019
1      2019
2      2019
3      2019
Name: dates, dtype: int64
```

Further Readings – Accessors

There are many other possible functions that can be called together with the accessors. The documentation of all possible methods for each accessor is present in these links for categorical, strings, and datetime.

7.3.2. DataFrame

Now that we understand the overall capabilities of the Pandas Series, we can simply define a DataFrame as a collection of Series. Think of it as a tabular (table-like) data structure that each column is expressed as a Series. Since tabular data is incredibly common, it is the most frequently used data structure in Pandas.

§ Creating DataFrame

Like in the Series, the creation function accepts multiple types of data as input. Beyond the **index** attribute, DataFrame has the **columns** attribute that can be passed during creation. The data can be passed as a dictionary with each key storing a list, list of series, list of lists, etc.

IPYTHON SHELL:

```
>>> dl = {'A':[1, 3], 'B': [2, 4]}
>>> pd.DataFrame(dl)                  # Dictionary of lists
   A  B
0  1  2
1  3  4

>>> lists = [[1,1], [2, 4]]
>>> pd.DataFrame(lists, columns=['A', 'B']) # List of lists
   A  B
0  1  2
1  3  4

>>> ds = {'A':pd.Series([1, 3]), 'B': pd.Series([2, 4])}
>>> pd.DataFrame(ds)                  # Dictionary of Series
   A  B
0  1  2
1  3  4

>>> s1 = pd.Series([1, 3, 5], index=[1, 2, 3])
>>> s2 = pd.Series([2, 4], index=[2, 3])
ds2 = {'A':s1, 'B': s2}
>>> pd.DataFrame(ds2)                 # Dictionary of Series
   A  B
1  1  NaN
2  3  2.0
3  5  4.0
```

OBS.: When using dictionaries of series, the indexes will be used to complete the DataFrame. Any value without value specified will be filled with "NaN".

§ Accessing Data and Operations

Similar to Series, DataFrames has multiple possible data access. In general, you can return another DataFrame or a Series when slicing the data.

```
IPYTHON SHELL:

>>> df = pd.DataFrame({'a':[1,2,3], 'b':[2,4,6], 'c':[1, 6, 9]})
>>> df
   a  b  c
0  1  2  1
1  2  4  6
2  3  6  9

>>> df[['a', 'b']]      # DataFrame view with selected cols
   a  c
0  1  1
1  2  6
2  3  9

>>> df['a']             # Return Series
0    1
1    2
2    3
Name: a, dtype: int64

>>> df.a                # Return Series (if columns name is str)
0    1
1    2
2    3
Name: a, dtype: int64
```

```
>>> df + 1              # Broadcasting
   a  b   c
0  2  3   2
1  3  5   7
2  4  7  10

>>>df.describe()        # Describing statistics
count  3.0  3.0  3.000000
mean   2.0  4.0  5.333333
std    1.0  2.0  4.041452
min    1.0  2.0  1.000000
25%    1.5  3.0  3.500000
50%    2.0  4.0  6.000000
75%    2.5  5.0  7.500000
max    3.0  6.0  9.000000
```

OBS.: When indexing columns and indexes, Pandas returns a view of the underlying DataFrame.

§ Displaying Values

Pandas DataFrame has two methods of displaying the begin/end of the tabular data: **head** and **tail**. This is useful when dealing with a large number or data.

```
IPYTHON SHELL:
>>> df = pd.DataFrame({'A':range(100), 'B':np.linspace(-5,
5, 100), 'C':0})
>>> df.head()                    # Default first 5  rows
      A          B  C
0     0 -5.000000  0
1     1 -4.898990  0
2     2 -4.797980  0
3     3 -4.696970  0
4     4 -4.595960  0

>>> df.tail(3)                   # Last 3 rows
      A          B  C
97   97  4.79798  0
98   98  4.89899  0
99   99  5.00000  0
```

7.3.3. Indexing, Slicing, and Iterating

We already saw some operations to access Pandas data structures. Furthermore, there are specific attributes to access Pandas DataFrame by position or column name.

§ loc and iloc

These attributes are used to access the data by position (**iloc**) or by index/column name (**loc**).

IPYTHON SHELL:

```
>>> df = pd.DataFrame({'a':[1,2,3], 'b':[2,4,6], 'c':[1, 6,
9]}, index=['i', 'j', 'k'])
>>> df
   a  b  c
i  1  2  1
j  2  4  6
k  3  6  9
>>> df.loc['i']        # Access all columns of row i by name
a    1
b    2
c    1
Name: i, dtype: int64

>>> df.loc[:, 'a']     # Access all rows of column a by name
i    1
j    2
k    3
Name: a, dtype: int64

>>> df.iloc[:, 2]      # Access 3rd columns by posisiton
i    1
j    6
k    9
Name: c, dtype: int64

>>> df.loc['k', 'b']   # Acces value by index/column name
6

>>> df.iloc[2, 1]      # Equivalent by index/column
6
```

§ Boolean Indexing

Pandas also supports **Boolean indexing**. As seen before, it is like Boolean indexing Numpy arrays. Therefore, **True** and **False** means if the value will be returned or not, respectively.

In general, they are used to perform filter operations on arrays, such as to get values above or below a given threshold. It works for **Series** of **DataFrames**. *And, or* and *not* can be represented by the operators &, | and ~, respectively. Pandas not only supports the **where** method that works like Boolean indexing, but also returns the not matching result as 'NaN' values.

IPYTHON SHELL:

```
>>> df = pd.DataFrame({'a':[1,2,3], 'b':[2,4,6], 'c':[1, 6,
9]}, index=['i', 'j', 'k'])

>>> df[df.a > 2]      # rows that column a is greater than 2
   a  b  c
k  3  6  9

>>> df[(df.a > 1) & (df.b < 5)] # rows where a > 1 and b <
5
   a  b  c
j  2  4  6

>>> df[(df.c <2) | (df.b < 5)]  # rows where c < 2 or b < 5
   a  b  c
i  1  2  1
j  2  4  6

>>> df[~(df.a == 2)]        # Rows where a is not equal to 2
   a  b  c
i  1  2  1
k  3  6  9

>>> df.where(df.a != 2)    # Similar, but return
                             not matching rows
      a    b    c
i   1.0  2.0  1.0
j   NaN  NaN  NaN
k   3.0  6.0  9.0
```

§ **Filter**

This method applies conditions to include the names of the specified axis. Therefore, it does not filter the content of the data but the labels of the indexes.

```
>>> df = pd.DataFrame({'ABC':[1,1,2], 'BCD':[0,1,3],
'CDE':[2, 1, 2]}, index=['dog', 'cat', 'rabbit'])
>>> df.filter(items=[«ABC», «CDE»])
                    # Select speficid columns
         ABC   CDE
dog       1     2
cat       1     1
rabbit    2     2

>>> df.filter(items=[«dog», «cat»], axis=0)
                    # Select speficid rows
        ABC   BCD   CDE
dog      1     0     2
cat      1     1     1

>>> df.filter(like=»BC»)  # Select columns that contains AB
         ABC   BCD
dog       1     0
cat       1     1
rabbit    2     3
```

7.4. **Combining DataFrames**

There are multiple possible ways to combine tabular data using Pandas. This topic will explore the most common ones of these types.

7.4.1. Merge

The function **pd.merge** can combine two DataFrames in one. In general, this function is used with these arguments: the first (left) and second (right) DataFrames, the type of merge, and columns that the DataFrames are being combined on. To better exemplify each case, consider DataFrames **df1** and **df2** defined below (empty cells represent missing values).

col1	col2
1	42
2	11
3	25

col1	col3
1	
2	22
4	51

The type of merge is passed to the parameter **how** that can be one of the following options:

- **left**: Use only keys from the left DataFrame in the result.

- **right**: Use only keys from the right DataFrame in the result.

- **outer**: Use the union of keys from the left and right DataFrames in the result.

- **inner**: Use the intersection of keys from the left and right DataFrame in the result.

These examples below give a better notion of the result.

```
IPYTHON SHELL:
>>> df1 = pd.DataFrame({"col1":[1, 2, 3],
"col2":[42,11,25]})
>>> df2 = pd.DataFrame({"col1":[1, 2, 4], "col3":[np.
nan,22,51]}

>>> pd.merge(df1, df2, how='left', on='col1')  # Left Merge
   col1  col2  col3
0     1    42   NaN
1     2    11  22.0
2     3    25   NaN

>>> pd.merge(df1, df2, how='right', on='col1') # Right Merge
   col1  col2  col3
0     1  42.0   NaN
1     2  11.0  22.0
2     4   NaN  51.0

>>> pd.merge(df1, df2, how='outer', on='col1') # Outer Merge
   col1  col2  col3
0     1  42.0   NaN
1     2  11.0  22.0
2     3  25.0   NaN
3     4   NaN  51.0
```

7.4.2. Concatenate

Once again, this is like concatenating Numpy arrays. Consider these examples shown in the IPython shell below.

IPYTHON SHELL:

```
>>> c1 = pd.DataFrame({"A":[1, 2, 3], "B":[42,11,25]})
>>> c2 = pd.DataFrame({"C":[1, 2, 4], "D":[np.nan,22,51]})

>>> pd.concat([c1, c2], axis=0)
     A     B    C     D
0  1.0  42.0  NaN   NaN
1  2.0  11.0  NaN   NaN
2  3.0  25.0  NaN   NaN
0  NaN   NaN  1.0   NaN
1  NaN   NaN  2.0  22.0
2  NaN   NaN  4.0  51.0

>>> pd.concat([c1, c2], axis=1)
   A   B  C     D
0  1  42  1   NaN
1  2  11  2  22.0
2  3  25  4  51.0
```

7.4.3. Grouping

Multiple times, you want to perform some aggregation functions in combined values. Using **groupby,** you can group a large amount of data and perform an operation on it. Grouping allows the calculation of some statistics such as mean, median, mode, standard deviation, etc. Consider the DataFrame, **df,** below.

breed	height	weight
Labrador	56	30
Labrador	60	29
Bulldog	40	24
Labrador	58	34
Beagle	36	11
Bulldog	38	22

Check the examples.

```
IPYTHON SHELL:
```

```
>>> df = pd.DataFrame({"breed":["Labrador",
"Labrador","Bulldog","Labrador", "Beagle", "Bulldog"],
"height":[57,60,40,58,36,38],"weight":[30,29,24,34,11,22]})
>>> df.groupby("breed").mean()   # Average height and weigh
          height  weight
breed
Beagle   36.000000    11.0
Bulldog  39.000000    23.0
Labrador 58.333333    31.0
>>> df.groupby("breed").min()     # Min height and weigh


         height  weight
breed
Beagle      36      11
Bulldog     38      22
Labrador    57      29


>>> df.groupby("breed").mean()   # Max height and weigh
         height  weight
breed
Beagle      36      11
Bulldog     40      24
Labrador    60      34
```

7.5. Data Cleaning

Pandas has multiple functions to perform data cleaning. It is a crucial step during data analysis and those functions facilitate the cleaning process.

7.5.1. Removing Missing Values

Series and DataFrame have extremely important methods called **dropna**, **isna**, and **fillna** to deal with missing values.

These methods have many arguments to remove/check or insert missing values from rows/columns. Consider the DataFrame, **df**, given.

A	B	C	D
		1	a
2	3.141	1	b
		2	
4	1.618	3	
	1.141	5	
6		8	

This **df** is used in the examples.

IPYTHON SHELL:

```
>>> df = pd.DataFrame({"A":[np.nan,2,np.nan,4,np.
nan,6], "B":[np.nan, 3.141,np.nan,1.618, 1.141, np.nan],
"C":[1,1,2,3,5,8], "D":["a","b",np.nan,np.nan,np.nan,np.
nan]})

>>> df.isna().sum()           # Total of missing values
                              #   per column
A    3
B    3
C    0
D    4
dtype: int64

>>> df.dropna()               # Drop all rows with
                              #   missing values
      A      B C D
1   2.0  3.141  1 b
>>> df.dropna(thresh=3)       # Drop all rows with <3
                              #   valid values
      A      B C    D
1   2.0  3.141  1    b
3   4.0  1.618  3  NaN
```

```
>>> df.dropna(how='all')          # Drop rows with all
                                     missing values
      A      B  C    D
0   NaN    NaN  1    a
1   2.0  3.141  1    b
2   NaN    NaN  2  NaN
3   4.0  1.618  3  NaN
4   NaN  1.141  5  NaN
5   6.0    NaN  8  NaN

>>> filler = {«A»:0, «B»:3.14, «D»:»?»}
>>> df.fillna(filler)             # Fill the missing values
      A      B  C  D
0   0.0  3.140  1  a
1   2.0  3.141  1  b
2   0.0  3.140  2  ?
3   4.0  1.618  3  ?
4   0.0  1.141  5  ?
5   6.0  3.140  8  ?
```

Further Readings – Missing Data

Pandas has a great documentation about dealing with missing data. The documentation explores more descriptive examples for each function and method.

7.5.2. Removing Duplicates

Pandas also has the capability of handling duplicates. Method **duplicated** and **drop_duplicates** deal with this type of data. Consider the DataFrame, **df**, below.

A	B	C	D
1	2	3	1
2	3	4	2
1	2	3	1
1	2	3	1
4	3	2	4

This **df** is used in the examples.

IPYTHON SHELL:

```
>>> df = pd.DataFrame({"A":[1,2,1,1,4],"B":[2, 3,2, 2,
3],"C":[3, 4 ,3, 3 ,2], "D":[1, 2, 1, 1, 4]})

>>> df.duplicated().sum()    # Total of duplicated rows
2


>>> df.drop_duplicates() # Drop all duplicated rows
A  B  C  D
0  1  2  3  1
1  2  3  4  2
4     4  3  2  4
```

Data Visualization

Data visualization is one of the finest ways to fully understand your data. **Python** has multiple libraries that can create great visualizations. In this chapter, we will present three of them: Matplotlib, for highly customizable graphs; Seaborn, for beautiful statistical graphs; and Bokeh, for dynamic graphs. Additionally, we will explore the plotting capabilities of the Pandas' package that uses Matplotlib in the background. In summary, this chapter presents different kinds of graphs, their roles representing different aspects of the data, and how to plot them on different packages.

8.1. Installing Packages

Using **pip,** run the command:

```
pip install pandas, matplotlib, seaborn, bokeh
```

With conda, just type:

```
conda install pandas, matplotlib, seaborn, bokeh
```

In general, these packages are imported with these aliases:

```
import pandas as pd
import matplotlib.pyplot as plt
import seaborn as sns
```

OBS.: Bokeh does not have a common alias to be imported, but in general explicit imports are used.

8.2. About the Packages

Some packages are better suited for representing specific plots than others. For instance, you can plot virtually any plot with Matplotlib. But some plots not implemented in this will require serious graphical knowledge and time. Some packages already provide a simpler solution for these graphs, and many of them use Matplotlib in the background (e.g., Seaborn and Pandas). Therefore, the examples of each kind of graph will only be represented in the most relevant packages. In general, these are the general characteristics of these packages:

o **Pandas and Matplotlib**: They can easily produce simple and yet useful graphs with minimal effort. Additionally, both can create graphs highly customized at the cost of simplicity.

o **Seaborn**: Beautiful and complex graphs related to statistical data. Contains various functions to plot difficult graphs in a simple and concise manner. However, the easy usage sacrifices customizability.

o **Bokeh**: A package that renders highly customizable dynamic plots on the browser or notebook. The customizability comes with the difficulty of use.

8.3. Charts/Graphs Objectives

Each chart has a purpose. They can be used to represent multiple information of one or multiple variables. In general, graphs can display four different aspects of the data/variables:

- Distribution;

- Composition;

- Comparison;

- Relationship.

We will go through the most common graphs on different packages and their purposes. To run any of the examples, consider that these packages were already imported. Any extra import is listed in the example itself.

EXAMPLES – DEFAULT IMPORTS

```
import matplootlib.pyplot as plt
import seaborn as sns
import pandas as pd
import numpy as np
from bokeh.plotting import figure, show
```

8.3.1. Histogram: Distribution

Simply put, the **Histogram** shows how the values of **one** variable are spread. The x-axis represents the values and the y-axis the frequency of these values (sometimes normalized). For a continuous variable is represented as an estimative of its probability distribution. It can be displayed in a discrete form (using bars that represent a certain range) or an approximated continuous line (simulates the distribution). The bar version can be easily displayed with Matplotlib and Pandas, and the continuous line using Seaborn. However, a dynamic histogram plot does not add much interesting detailed information that justifies the dynamic plot.

§ EXAMPLES

EXAMPLES - MATPLOTLIB, PANDAS AND SEABORN

```python
# Data
data = np.random.normal(size=1000)

# Matplotlib
plt.hist(data)
plt.show()

# Pandas
data_series = pd.Series(data)
data_series.hist()
plt.show()
# Seaborn
sns.distplot(data)
plt.show()
```

OUTPUT - MATPLOTLIB AND PANDAS (SAME OUTPUT)

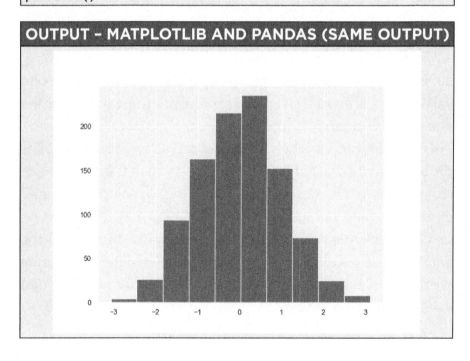

OUTPUT - SEABORN

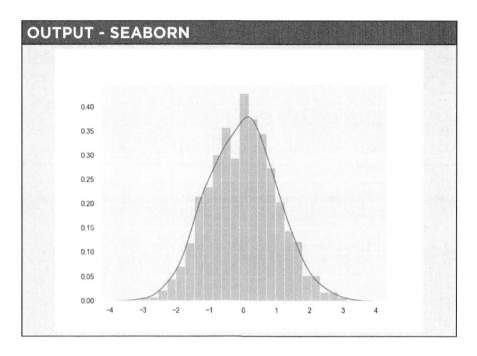

8.3.2. Box Plot: Distribution

The box plot is a useful plot to extract statistical information of **one** variable. It is represented by a box with a centerline and two prolonged "arms." The middle line represents the mean value, and the box length is in the first and third quartiles of the data. The points outside the extended lines are considered outliers. It has many variations implemented on Seaborn. Some variations have more details, such as a **boxen** plot, while others add more distribution information at the cost of statistical values. Examples are **swarm** and **violin** plot. Pandas and Matplotlib have a simple function to plot box plots, but Bokeh does not.

Further Readings – Bokeh Box Plot

Even though Bokeh does not have a direct function to plot a Box plot, it is completely possible to create this plot. By the way, a box plot is one of the plots in their gallery. Look at the example and try to understand what is happening. Similar things are done behind the curtains when using the functions of the other packages.

EXAMPLES – MATPLOTLIB, PANDAS AND SEABORN

```
# Data
data = np.random.normal(size=1000)

# Matplotlib
plt.boxplot(data)
plt.show()

# Pandas
data_series = pd.Series(data)
data_series.plot(kind='box')
plt.show()

# Seaborn
sns.swarmplot(data)
plt.show()
sns.violinplot(data)
plt.show()
sns.boxenplot(data)
plt.show()
```

OUTPUT - MATPLOTLIB AND PANDAS (SAME OUTPUT)

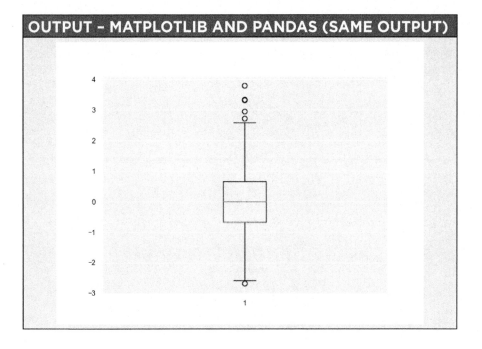

OUTPUTS - SEABORN

8.3.3. Scatter Plot: Distribution and Relationship

This simple chart provides a lot of info about **two** variables of the data, how these variables are distributed with one another, and possibly their relationship (e.g., increase together). As the histogram, it represents how these variables are spread. The x-axis represents the values of the first variable, the y-axis the values of the second variable for each entry in the data. It has some variations, such as **hexbin** and **estimateddensity** plots, where the frequency of the points in a region is represented by the color intensity. Once again, the simple scatter plot can be easily displayed with Matplotlib and Pandas, and the fancier equivalents **hexbin** and **estimateddensity** using Seaborn. This type of plot is where the advantages of dynamics plot with Bokeh become incredibly useful. For example, dynamic scatter plots make outliers easily detectable and allow easy inspection.

EXAMPLES - MATPLOTLIB, PANDAS, SEABORN AND BOKEH

```
# Data
data = np.random.normal(size=(1000, 2))

# Matplotlib
plt.plot(data[:, 0], data[:, 1])
plt.show()

# Pandas
data_df = pd.DataFrame(data, columns=['a', 'b'])
data_df.plot(x='a', y='b', kind='scatter')
plt.show()

# Seaborn
sns.jointplot(data[:, 0], data[:, 1], kind='hex')
plt.show()
sns.jointplot(data[:, 0], data[:, 1], kind='kde')
plt.show()

# Bokeh
p = figure()
p.circle(data[:, 0], data[:, 1])
show(p)
```

OUTPUT – MATPLOTLIB AND PANDAS (SAME OUTPUT)

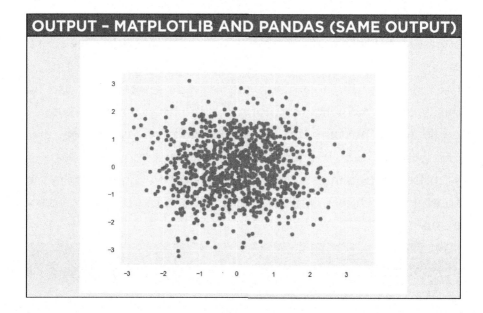

OUTPUTS - SEABORN

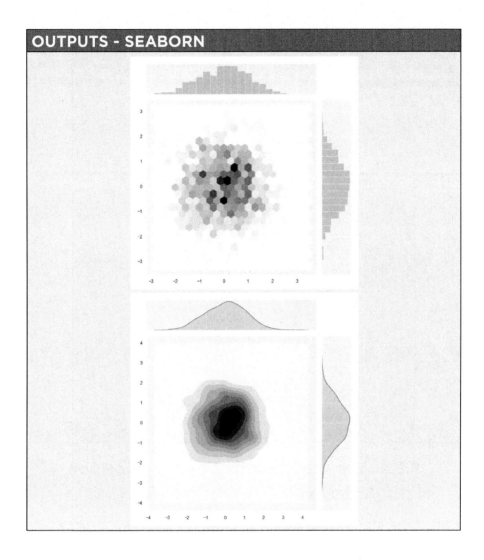

OUTPUTS - BOKEH

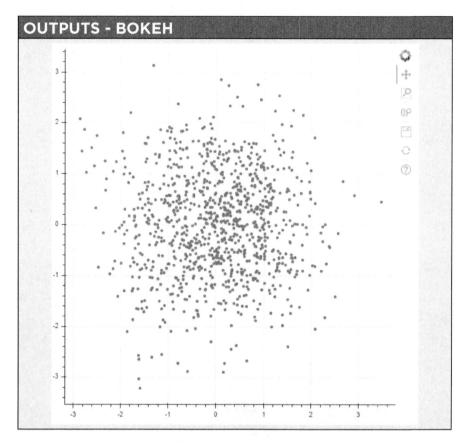

8.3.4. Bar Plot: Distribution, Composition and Comparison

Bar plots are widely used to compare numerical variables with categorical ones, or to represent the distribution or composition of categorical variables. Each bar represents a category, and the bar length represents a numerical value that can be a statistical value (number of occurrences of the categorical variable) or another numerical variable being associated. This graph has vertical and horizontal versions, the latter one is used for categories with longer names. This is one of the simplest and meaningful plots and can be easily displayed with any of the libraries.

EXAMPLES –
MATPLOTLIB, PANDAS, SEABORN AND BOKEH

```python
# Data
fruits = [«apple», «banana», «grape», «strawberry»,
«papaya»]
data = np.random.choice(fruits, size=100)
count_values = pd.Series(data).value_counts()
# Matplotlib
plt.plot(count_values.index,count_values.values)
plt.show()

# Pandas
count_values.plot(kind='bar')
plt.show()

# Seaborn
sns.barplot(count_values.index,count_values.values)
plt.show()

# Bokeh
p = figure(x_range=list(count_values.index))
p.vbar(x=count_values.index, top=count_values.values,
width=.9)
show(p)
```

OUTPUT - MATPLOTLIB

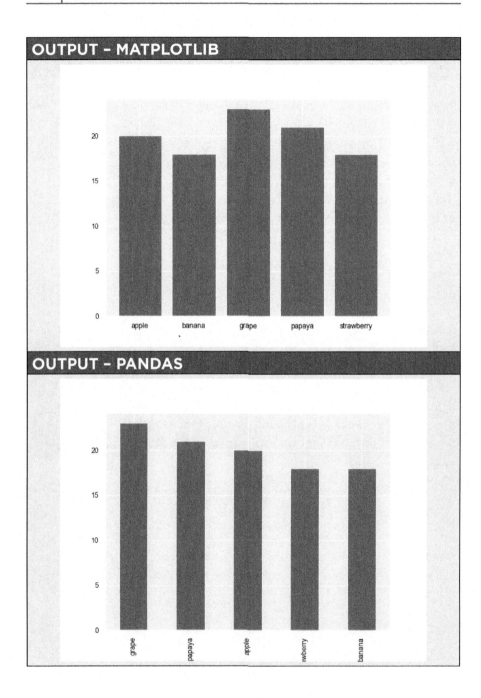

OUTPUT - PANDAS

OUTPUTS - SEABORN

OUTPUTS - BOKEH

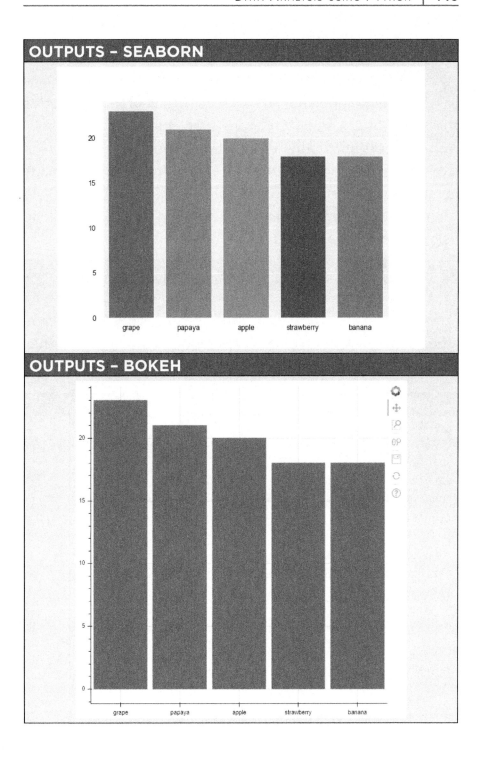

8.3.5. Pie Plot: Composition

When using pie plots (also known as pizza plots), the goal is to represent composition. Each "slice" of the graph represents the value of a certain category that composes the whole. Another version of this chart is the Doughnut plot, which is essentially a pie plot without the center part. Not many libraries provide simple support to pie charts since bar plots are more common alternatives. Below, the plots were done using Matplotlib and Pandas.

Further Readings – The issue with pie chart

It is arguable that the pie plot is an efficient way to represent composition. This <u>post</u> discusses its downsides. Also, read the comment section that brings important cases where the pie chart seems a great fit.

EXAMPLES – MATPLOTLIB, PANDAS

```
# Data
fruits = [«apple», «banana», «grape», «strawberry»,
«papaya»]
data = np.random.choice(fruits, size=100)
count_values = pd.Series(data, name=»fruits»).value_
counts()

# Matplotlib
plt.pie(count_values.values, labels=count_values.index)
plt.show()

# Pandas
count_values.plot(kind='pie')
plt.show()
```

OUTPUT –
MATPLOTLIB AND PANDAS (SAME OUTPUT)

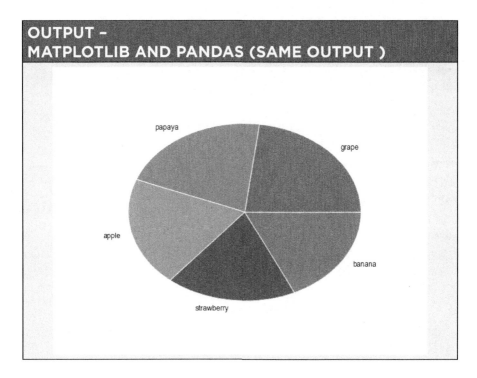

8.3.6. Line Plot: Comparison

Line charts are used to compare how a numerical variable changes with another numerical variable (in general, a temporal one). They are like scatter plots but with a connection between the points. They are highly customizable with different markers, line effects, and colors. All libraries provide simple support to this type of chart.

EXAMPLES – MATPLOTLIB, PANDAS, SEABORN, AND BOKEH

```python
# Data
x = np.arange(100)
y = np.random.normal(size=100) + 5*np.sin(x/20)

# Matplotlib
plt.plot(x, y)
plt.show()

# Pandas
pd.Series(y).plot()
plt.show()

# Seaborn
sns.barplot(count_values.index,count_values.values)
plt.show()

# Bokeh
p = figure()
p.line(x=count_values.index, top=count_values.values,
width=.9)
show(p)
```

OUTPUT – MATPLOTLIB, PANDAS, AND SEABORN (SIMILAR OUTPUT)

OUTPUT – BOKEH

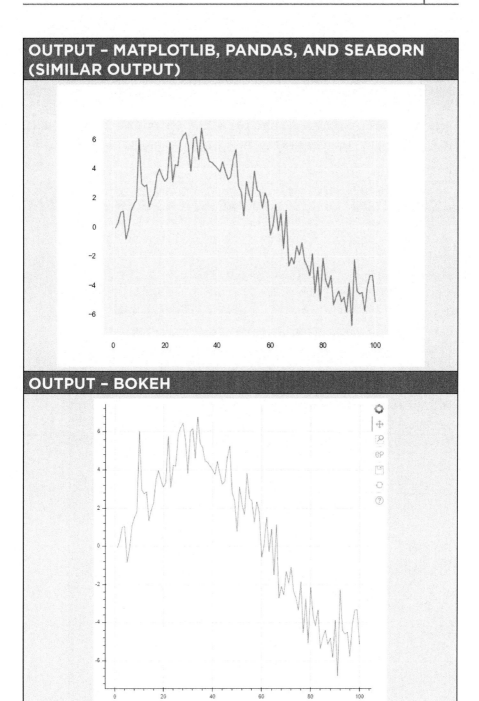

8.3.7. Heatmaps: Relationship

This graph combines two categorical variables with a numerical value that can represent a rating or information between them. The numerical value modifies the intensity of the color representing a stronger or weaker relationship. Simple support is only provided by the Seaborn library.

EXAMPLES – SEABORN
```
# Data
fruits = [«apple», «banana», «grape», «strawberry»,
«papaya»]
stage = [«ripe», «unripe», «rooten»]

data_fruits = np.random.choice(fruits, size=100)
data_stage = np.random.choice(stage, size=100)
ct = pd.crosstable(data_fruits, data_stage)

# Seaborn
sns.heatmap(ct)
plt.show()
```

OUTPUT –
MATPLOTLIB AND PANDAS (SAME OUTPUT)

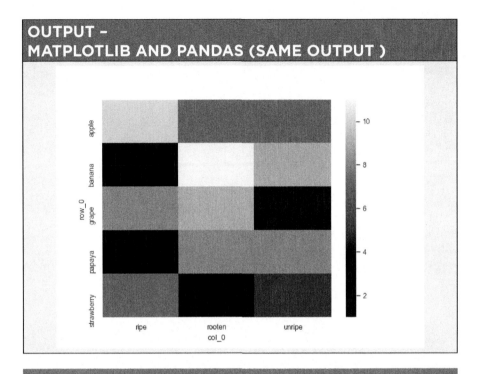

Hands-on Time –Quick Guides

There are three notebooks with Quick Guider on how to get started on all three of those libraries. Go through the notebook and experiment, creating beautiful custom graphs using these packages.

Thanks, Data Scientist and Python Programmer

Congrats on completing this book. You now have an elementary understanding of the main concepts of Python for data analysis.

If you want to help us produce more material like this, then please leave an honest review online. It really does make a difference.

If you have any feedback, kindly let us know by sending an email to contact@aispublishing.net.

Your feedback is highly valued. At AI Publishing, we are genuinely excited about hearing from you. It will be very helpful for us to improve the quality of our books.

Until next time, happy analyzing.

From the
Same Publisher

Printed in Great Britain
by Amazon

13803675R00099